A Student's Guide to

GEORGE
ORWELL

Titles in the **UNDERSTANDING LITERATURE** *Series*:

A Student's Guide to
EMILY DICKINSON
0-7660-2285-4

A Student's Guide to
F. SCOTT FITZGERALD
0-7660-2202-1

A Student's Guide to
NATHANIEL HAWTHORNE
0-7660-2283-8

A Student's Guide to
ERNEST HEMINGWAY
0-7660-2431-8

A Student's Guide to
ARTHUR MILLER
0-7660-2432-6

A Student's Guide to
WILLIAM SHAKESPEARE
0-7660-2284-6

A Student's Guide to
JOHN STEINBECK
0-7660-2259-5

UNDERSTANDING
LITERATURE

A Student's Guide to

GEORGE
ORWELL

A. L. Means

Enslow Publishers, Inc.

40 Industrial Road	PO Box 38
Box 398	Aldershot
Berkeley Heights, NJ 07922	Hants GU12 6BP
USA	UK

http://www.enslow.com

Library of Congress Cataloging-in-Publication Data

Means, Andrew L.
    A student's guide to George Orwell / Andrew L. Means
        p. cm. — (Understanding literature)
    Includes bibliographical references and index.
    ISBN 0-7660-2433-4
    1. Orwell, George, 1903–1950—Criticism and interpretation—Handbooks,
manuals, etc. 2. Satire, English—History and criticism—Handbooks, manuals,
etc. 3. Dystopias in literature—Handbooks, manuals, etc.—Juvenile literature.
I. Title. II. Series.
    PR6029.R8Z7355 2005
    828'.91209—dc22

                                  2005010169

Printed in the United States of America

10 9 8 7 6 5 4 3 2 1

To Our Readers:
We have done our best to make sure all Internet Addresses in this book were active
and appropriate when we went to press. However, the author and the publisher
have no control over and assume no liability for the material available on those
Internet sites or on other Web sites they may link to. Any comments or suggestions
can be sent by e-mail to comments@enslow.com or to the address on the back
cover.

Illustration Credits: AP/ Wide World Photos, pp. 18, 77, 120; Art Today,
Inc., pp. 24, 34; Library of Congress, p. 85.

Cover Illustration: AP/ Wide World Photos (inset); Corel Corporation/
Hemera Technologies, Inc./ Art Today, Inc. (background objects).

CONTENTS

THE LIFE OF A WRITER

An Introduction to the Life and Works of George Orwell

Most lives can be seen from several viewpoints, and this is especially true of writers. By the very nature of their work, writers tend to be complicated studies. What they write may contradict what they say or do in their private lives, leaving readers with ideas about them that are very different ideas from those held by families, friends, or literary colleagues. In addition, writers' opinions and interests may change dramatically, depending on their experiences or the influence of others. Also, their work may go in and out of fashion throughout their careers and even after their deaths.

In other words, a writer leaves a trail in this respect. George Orwell, more than most, left a powerful record of his beliefs and feelings. There may be contradictions and hypocrisies in the course of his life and writing, but few

CAPITALISM—*An economic system in which private individuals and corporations own the means of producing and distributing goods and services and play a major part in controlling wealth.*

COMMUNISM—*A political system of common ownership planned and controlled by the state, based on the Marxist doctrine of revolution by the working class, or proletariat, against capitalism.*

PROTAGONIST— *The main character in a work of fiction.*

other people have been as outspoken and consistent in voicing their core convictions.

From his early days as a writer, Orwell established his theme: opposition to oppressive hierarchies that seek to limit individual freedoms. In this he was as outspoken in condemning the unfairness of capitalism and the class system in his native Great Britain as he was in preaching against the excesses of communism.

The theme took shape in his early novels, which focus on the struggle of his protagonists—the central characters—against convention. It had much to do with his writing about social conditions among the poor in England and Paris and about the Spanish Civil War of 1936–39. Ultimately, of course, it led to his attacks on totalitarianism in his last two books, *Animal Farm* and *1984*.

WHY ORWELL WROTE

Orwell left no doubt about his motivation for becoming a writer. He analyzed the output of many writers in book reviews and essays, and was just as forthcoming about his own work. A principal source of information is Orwell's 1946 essay "Why I Write," which begins with the declaration that he wanted to be a writer from "a very early age, perhaps the age of five or six."[1]

TOTALITARIANISM— *A form of government in which the authorities seek to exercise complete control over every aspect of life and tolerate no opposition.*

"I knew that I had a facility with words and a power of facing unpleasant facts," he continued, "and I felt that this created a sort of private world in which I could get my own back for my failure in everyday life."[2]

His first composition, he recollected, was a poem about a tiger, written when he was about four and probably based on William Blake's famous poem, "The Tyger." When he was about sixteen, he read John Milton's saga, *Paradise Lost*, and "suddenly discovered the joy of mere words." He dreamed of devising "enormous naturalistic novels with unhappy endings, full of detailed descriptions and arresting similes, and also full of purple passages in which words were used partly for the sake of their sound."[3]

SIMILE—*A comparison, usually with "like" or "as," in which the thing being described is understood better by being compared to something with similar qualities.*

Then followed a period of several years when Orwell's focus was diverted away from this calling to be a writer. In Burma he kept up with the distant literary world as well as he could through magazines and whatever novels he could acquire. Not until his return to England in 1927 was he able to devote himself to writing.

SOCIALISM—*A political system in which the community shares power on a relatively equal basis and the state owns means of making and distributing goods. In Marxist theory, the stage that societies go through between capitalism and communism.*

There are four main motives for writing prose, Orwell stated in "Why I Write": "sheer egoism," "esthetic enthusiasm," "historical impulse," and "political purpose." In a more peaceful era, he said, he would by nature be more inclined toward the first three. He would be motivated by building his reputation, by the pleasure of writing, and by the "historical impulse" of researching facts and circumstances.[4] Only because of his exposure to colonialism in Burma and working class conditions on his return to England had he become an advocate of political and social change. Belief in socialism gave him a sense of purpose that went beyond merely expressing his personality in print.

When he was not clear about what he wanted to say, he thought, his work was lifeless, "betrayed into purple passages, sentences without meaning, decorative adjectives." Orwell's focus was on writing clearly ("Good prose is like a window pane,") and meaningfully instead of trying to be clever with words and images.[5] This did not necessarily make the work of writing easy though. The creative process still had an element of mystery about it.

"Writing a book is a horrible, exhausting struggle, like a long bout of some painful illness," he explained. "One would never undertake such a thing if one were not driven on by some demon whom one can neither resist nor understand."[6]

POLITICAL CONTENT

Politics and writing are almost inseparable in Orwell's career. His first published novel, *Burmese Days*, took aim at colonial rule. Political and economic trends of the 1930s kept his attention on the lives of oppressed and deprived people. What he saw of poverty and inequality during his travels helped turn him into a socialist, and his experiences fighting in Spain strengthened his convictions.

In one of his final essays, "Writers And Leviathan" (1948), Orwell discussed the demands placed on writers by politics. In the modern world, he felt, it was no longer possible for writers to be politically detached. The urgent need Orwell felt to defeat totalitarianism in Europe and improve conditions for the working classes is reflected in the simplicity he favored in his writing. At the same time, writers must not become propagandists and must be candid in what they write, even if it sometimes conflicts with their political allegiances.

PROPAGANDIST— *Having to do with propaganda; someone who spreads propaganda.*

Orwell's ideas about social and political issues took precedence over development of plot and character. He was not a master of building suspense or keeping the reader guessing about the direction of a story. His descriptions of people and places tend to give no more detail than necessary for continuity. For the most part, detours from the main narrative are restricted. An exception to

PROPAGANDA— *Facts, ideas, and rumors that are spread for the purpose of advancing some political aim or cause.*

this is the use of flashbacks in his fourth novel, *Coming Up For Air*, in which the recollections of the main character, George Bowling, drive the entire story.

LITERARY DEVICES

The literary device that has done the most to build Orwell's reputation is satire, notably in *Animal Farm*. This relatively simple story exposes Soviet tyranny more memorably than a detailed history could have done. Satire was ideally suited to the time and the subject. *Animal Farm* also shows how Orwell could be ironic sometimes, making statements not intended to be understood at face value.

SATIRE—*A literary work which exposes vice or folly by making fun of it.*

USE OF LANGUAGE

As might be expected from the writer who coined the term "Newspeak" in *1984*, Orwell was very concerned with word use. In his later work, he tried to eliminate "decorative adjectives" and "purple passages"—in other words, description that was not essential to the story.[7] He put some of his thoughts on the subject into his essay "Politics and the English Language."

IRONY—*A word or phrase used with the intention of conveying a meaning different from the literal one, often with the idea of ridiculing the literal meaning.*

Clear thinking, he argued, results from precise and concise use of language. Slovenly use of words, he wrote, makes it easier to have foolish thoughts. He singled out for criticism metaphors that have become clichés and words and phrases that are more complicated than necessary. Never use foreign or scientific words or jargon, he advised, if there is an everyday English equivalent.

NEWSPEAK—*A version of the English language introduced by the ruling party in* 1984 *and intended to control people's thoughts by restricting vocabulary.*

BIOGRAPHICAL DETAILS IN ORWELL'S FICTION

METAPHOR—*A word or phrase used in a nonliteral way in order to suggest a comparison between the thing described and its symbolic qualities.*

As novelists tend to do, George Orwell borrowed liberally from his own life for his stories. Plots and characters drew from his experiences, people he knew, and attitudes and opinions he had formed. Of course, he also actively looked for material, especially through his travels.

Orwell's first novel, *Burmese Days*, clearly derives from his service as a police officer in Burma. His growing disillusionment with colonialism fueled the book's main character, John Flory.

Orwell's jobs as a school teacher and, briefly, as a crop harvester gave him material for his second novel, *A Clergyman's Daughter*. In *Keep the Aspidistra*

JARGON—*Words, phrases, or abbreviations understood in a specialized field but often meaningless to the general population.*

Flying, he imposed his own attitudes about money and sex on the protagonist, Gordon Comstock, who also worked in a bookstore—as did Orwell for a short time. *Coming Up for Air* is based largely on his recollections of growing up in a country town.

Similarities with his own life are fewer in *Animal Farm*, as would be expected from the allegorical nature of the story. The original name for the farm, Manor Farm, had a namesake near Orwell's cottage in the village of Wallington. But it was a common name for an English farm in any case.

ALLEGORY—*A story in which characters and events represent ideas, principles, or forces, so that there is a symbolic meaning in what takes place.*

Perhaps the most notable biographical input in *1984* stems from using some of his second wife's characteristics for Julia.[8] But the story also incorporates impressions from his time working at the BBC, ranging from physical surroundings to use of language. Orwell's fascination with rats, which was noted even by a comrade in the Spanish trenches, has a small but significant role too.[9]

Above all, Orwell's work was shaped by the times in which he lived. Coming into adulthood in the 1920s, he was deeply affected by the social and political changes between the two world wars. Among the most important of these was the Russian Revolution, which initially was regarded as a model by many reformers and idealists in other countries. It was many years before Stalin's tyranny would be seen in a harsher light. Orwell would become one of the foremost critics of Stalin.

At the same time, Orwell felt that many people were oppressed by the combination of capitalism and empire in his own country. He had seen how the Burmese people were treated by their British rulers. When he returned to England, he wrote about the terrible living conditions experienced by many working class people. As his political philosophy matured, he balanced a belief in democracy with a feeling that true equality of opportunity and material well-being would be best achieved through socialism.

ATTITUDE TOWARD JEWS, WOMEN, AND HOMOSEXUALS

Orwell was a man of his time, place, and upbringing, and he inherited many old-fashioned and now unacceptable views. Some critics have accused him of being anti-Semitic and having a low opinion of women and homosexuals.[10]

References to Jews in his early books, *Down and Out in Paris and London* and *Burmese Days*, seem hostile. On the other hand, the leader of the opposition to Big Brother in *1984* is Jewish. Orwell also wrote an essay in 1945, entitled "Antisemitism In Britain," about the irrational basis for prejudice against Jews. His viewpoint changed with events, notably the Holocaust and the postwar creation of Israel.

His central female characters cannot be described as

deep thinkers. Even the rebellious Julia in *1984* falls asleep during a political discussion. Likewise, their male companions are not particularly enlightened. They tend to see women predominantly in sexual terms, or at least with a patronizing air of superiority.

"He wanted to be attractive to women but found he was not, and seems to have been punishing them for that for the rest of his life," claimed one of Orwell's biographers.[11]

LITERARY INFLUENCES

Some of the fiction writers in the generations immediately preceding his own must have seemed self-indulgent and sentimental to Orwell in his adult years. Turn-of-the-twentieth-century writers like Rudyard Kipling (*The Jungle Book, Kim*) and childhood favorites like Kenneth Grahame (*The Wind in the Willows*) portrayed an idyllic world, or at least one remote from the suffering and repression gripping Europe in the late 1920s and 1930s. Even H.G. Wells (*The Time Machine, The War of the Worlds*), with his optimistic view of technological advances and social improvements, he regarded as out of touch.

From his school days, Orwell was a dedicated reader. He did not confine himself to books in English either. The French writers Flaubert and Maupassant were apparently favorites. Inevitably, Orwell must have been influenced by what he read.

Among writers Orwell credited as influences through

his reading were Somerset Maugham, a leading literary figure of the preceding generation, and a relatively obscure late-Victorian novelist, George Gissing. Orwell admired Maugham, he noted in a 1940 autobiographical sketch, "for his power of telling a story straightforwardly and without frills."[12] Gissing had struggled to make a living from writing, and only began to find some success as a novelist when he was dying of tuberculosis. Orwell was drawn to these similarities with his own life, according to a couple of his friends.[13]

Like Gordon Comstock in *Keep the Aspidistra Flying*, Orwell also wrote poetry. As a young man, he exchanged verses with a girlfriend, and poems sometimes appear in his books and essays. One of his best known, included in his essay "Why I Write," is very much in keeping with his notion that writers are products of their times. He might have been a "happy vicar" in a more peaceful era, he mused, concluding that he was not suited to such troubled times—and nor, he implied was anyone else.[14] However, any idea of basing his career on poetry apparently did not last long.

CRITIQUES OF WRITERS

Orwell's essays give many insights into his thinking and experiences. His topics are mostly politics, popular culture, and literature, although he also used his essays to reflect on his personal life.

Among the literary subjects of Orwell's critiques are

Born Eric Arthur Blair in India in 1903, Blair would eventually gain worldwide fame writing under the name George Orwell.

Mark Twain, Leo Tolstoy, W. B. Yeats, and Jonathan Swift. Orwell was a great admirer of Swift, whose *Gulliver's Travels* has been a model for satirical allegory since it was written in the early eighteenth century.

Of course, Orwell's views of other writers were colored by his and their politics. He could admire their writing talents sometimes and yet disapprove of their vision or, as he saw it, lack of vision. In this respect, he enjoyed the work of Kipling and Charles Dickens, and yet criticized their opinions. While noting the vitality in Kipling's work, Orwell disapproved of his support of British imperialism. Dickens, Orwell felt, did not appreciate the need for a political restructuring of society even though he wrote vivid descriptions of individuals experiencing hard times. With a memorable metaphor, Orwell described Dickens' writing as "rotten architecture, but wonderful gargoyles."[15]

In the same essay, he made an amusing comparison between the writers of Dickens' era and those of his own. Whatever their faults, the earlier writers showed a familiarity with the society in which they lived, Orwell allowed, whereas "a writer nowadays is so hopelessly isolated that the typical modern novel is a novel about a novelist."[16]

More insight into Orwell's influences and ideas about writing comes from another essay, "Inside The Whale." It begins with comments about the American writer Henry Miller and his book about the artistic life in Paris in the mid-1930s, *Tropic of Cancer*. Although Miller's lack of political concerns was so different from his own viewpoint, Orwell clearly was intrigued by the novel. He rated its attention to graphic detail nearly as highly as that of another influential volume, James Joyce's *Ulysses*.

CHILDHOOD HEROES AND CONTEMPORARIES

One of Orwell's earliest inspirations was A.E. Housman, whose poem "A Shropshire Lad" was a great favorite. Orwell recalled reciting it "in a kind of ecstasy."[17] The poem was written at the end of the nineteenth century, when country images were popular. As Orwell went to great lengths to illustrate, the place and time in which a writer works has much to do with the prose or poetry produced. Housman was followed by a generation immersed in the violent imagery of World War I. This, in turn, gave way to a period, according to Orwell, in which writers were out of touch with the events of their time. The implications of the Russian Revolution, for example, were ignored in favor of what Orwell felt were obscure and unrealistic personal obsessions. He singled out D.H. Lawrence, whose candor about sex and relationships had scandalized many during the three decades before "Inside The Whale" was published in 1940. (While Orwell did not approve of Lawrence's focus on intensely personal subject matter, he did admire Lawrence's writing style.)

With the arrival of the 1930s, Orwell detected more of a sense of purpose in contemporary literature. By this he seems to have meant a willingness to comment on, and make judgments about, social and political issues—not that he was always in agreement with the views expressed.

"Nearly all the dominant writers of the thirties," he wrote, "belonged to the soft-boiled emancipated middle class."[18] In his opinion, some had supported Europe's communist and fascist regimes without knowing what they were talking about. Writers, he warned, should carefully consider their political involvements. Faced with the complexities of the 1930s, it was easy to be misled.

FASCISM—*A political system in which the state controls virtually every aspect of how people live, suppressing opposition, emphasizing conservative values, and typically acting aggressively toward other nations.*

ORWELL THE MAN

Orwell was a complex man, whose personality and politics were sometimes in conflict. An eccentric individualist, he might have found it hard to adjust to the structured society he advocated as a committed socialist. By nature, it seems, he mistrusted mass movements.

What his output and life would have been like if he had lived past the age of forty-six is a matter for speculation. Orwell himself apparently said he had more books in him. However, there is no doubt about the legacy he did leave. Terms he coined are now part of our language. The political allegories he created are indispensable for an understanding of the modern world. As a result, his name and work are known and revered worldwide.

HIS LIFE
AND
WORK

Influences on George Orwell

I f there were a prize for coining the most memorable political slogan of the last century, author George Orwell would be a strong contender. Even people who have not read his two best known books, *1984* and *Animal Farm*, recognize the menace in the warning "Big Brother is watching you."

Big Brother, *1984*'s all-powerful political figurehead, is one of the most evocative images in literature. Like the novel's main character, Winston Smith, the reader is led to question whether Big Brother is a real person or a mythical being. All we know for certain, for much of the book anyway, is that in the name of Big Brother the political system strives to control the thoughts and actions of every citizen. Big Brother demands absolute conformity and loyalty.

No wonder Orwell was able to conceive of such a nightmare. He based his ideas for both *1984* and *Animal Farm* on what was happening in the world around him. In the persons of the dictators Adolf Hitler and Joseph Stalin, he had ideal models for his work. Orwell lived in the first half of the twentieth century, in an era of

BIG BROTHER— *The mythical, all-knowing leader of the state of Oceania in Orwell's novel* 1984.

profound political change, and his writing reflects the dilemmas, hopes, and pitfalls of that time. Fascists and communists were fighting the established order and each other for control of Europe. Orwell himself fought for several months with an anarchist militia in one of the early struggles between these ideologies, in the Spanish Civil War of 1936–1939.

Even though we are long past *1984*, the year in which his futuristic novel was set, Orwell's concept of a state that manipulates its inhabitants to the point that they become like zombies has never lost

ANARCHISM—*The theory or doctrine that all forms of government are oppressive and undesirable and should be abolished.*

its validity. Big Brother may have been based on Soviet leader Joseph Stalin and Nazi Germany's Adolph Hitler, but in today's world, with its electronic eavesdropping and security cameras, the potential for abuse of power is just as real and immediate. Perhaps even more so.

Orwell's main theme of oppression by various social and political systems was reinforced by his experiences at school, as a young man living in Burma, and then as a transient in Paris and London. After he fought in the Spanish Civil War, his ideas matured into the viewpoint that led to his great works about political tyranny, *Animal Farm* and *1984*.

Security cameras like the one above remind Orwell fans around the world of the famous slogan, "Big Brother is watching you."

EARLY LIFE

George Orwell was born Eric Arthur Blair on June 25, 1903, in Motihari, a village in Bengal, India. His father, Richard, was a minor official in the British civil service in India and met his mother, Ida, there. Both sides of the family included members working in colonial capacities in India and Burma, which were then part of the British Empire.

The Blairs could lay claim to an aristocratic British heritage, but they had descended into a more modest middle-class way of life by the time Eric was born. His grandfather, Thomas Blair, was a clergyman who served in India and other British territories.

When he was still a toddler, Eric returned with his mother and older sister Marjorie to England. With their father a rare visitor from his posting in India, the family lived in the town of Henley on the River Thames. Orwell recalled his father as "a gruff-voiced elderly man forever saying 'Don't.'"[1] At the age of five—just about the time another sister, Avril, was born—he started attending a convent school.

Three years later Orwell transferred to a boarding school called St. Cyprian's, on England's south coast. Then, in his early teens, he won a scholarship to Eton, one of the country's most prestigious schools.

Orwell was already showing signs of being a maverick. Apparently he was not a very good student, spending more time on his own reading rather than on the school curriculum.

In an essay, published thirty years later, he wrote that being an author was his goal from an early age. "I had the lonely child's habit of making up stories and holding conversations with imaginary persons," he revealed, "and I think from the very start my literary ambitions were mixed up with the feeling of being isolated and undervalued."[2]

This background helps explain why, as a mature writer, Orwell was drawn to the poor and dispossessed for so much of the material for his essays and novels. Evidently he did not enjoy much about his school days. In

"Such, Such Were The Joys," an essay published after his death, Orwell described conditions at St. Cyprian's (disguised as "Crossgates" in the essay) as "overcrowded" and the boys as "underfed, underwashed."[3] He had been taken out of the "warm nest" of home, he wrote, and "flung into a world of force and fraud and secrecy."[4]

Matters were made worse by his poor health—Orwell suffered from a bronchial complaint, he wrote—and by the snobbishness and bullying he experienced both from other boys and his teachers. Some former St. Cyprian's students have suggested that Orwell exaggerated the horrors of life there.

At Eton, Orwell had more freedom and dignity. Still, his school days seem to have led him into a lifelong obsession about authoritarian systems, whether educational or political, and how they can suppress the individual. As a boy, he felt powerless against teachers and bullies, and endured punishments and indignities with a fatalistic acceptance of the status quo. As an adult, he wrote about comparable circumstances in a political context.

Typically, boys at Eton were expected to go on to university. Orwell chose instead to follow his forefathers into colonial service by joining the police in Burma. Later, this part of his life became the basis of his novel *Burmese Days*.

His Career As A Writer

At the beginning of 1928, back home from southeast Asia on leave, Orwell resigned from the police and devoted himself to writing.[5] The first book published was the autobiographical *Down and Out in Paris and London*, a manifesto for his growing conviction that British capitalism and imperialism exploited the working classes as well as the colonies. During this period, he adopted his pen name, George Orwell, apparently in order to shield his family from his emerging reputation as a radical.

By this time his physical appearance had changed too. Longtime associates commented on how much he had aged in Burma, and photos indicate as much. His face seemed flat and angular, and was dominated by a thin moustache, deep-set eyes, and thick, dark hair curling above his forehead. He was relatively tall, and tended to stand out in groups. There was a "gauntness" about his looks, remembered his friend George Woodcock. But, when he smiled, "unexpected kindliness would irradiate his whole face."[6]

Orwell was not able to find a publisher for *Down and Out* at first, and so began writing his second book, *Burmese Days*. Eventually, when *Down and Out* was published in 1933, it established his credentials as a social and political commentator.

Burmese Days, published in 1934 in the United States and the following year in Britain, was loosely based on his experiences in the police. Drawing from the same source, he wrote two shorter pieces in the early thirties that indicated he would be a persuasive essayist. "A Hanging" was about an execution and "Shooting an Elephant" described an incident in which Orwell apparently was forced to kill a rampaging elephant. Two novels came next: *A Clergyman's Daughter* (1935) and *Keep the Aspidistra Flying* (1936). Both continued his focus on the theme of class.

The year 1936 was an eventful one both for Orwell's personal life and his career. In January he visited the industrial areas of northern England to research social and work conditions. The resulting book, *The Road to Wigan Pier*, has come to be regarded as one of his most significant. In addition to graphic detail of mining life, Orwell once again delved into analysis of class and socialism. His research profoundly affected his views on what needed to be done about poverty and inequality. Reportedly, his descriptions were a revelation to some readers who had no direct contact with Britain's mining communities. Typically, his critique did not toe the conventional socialist line. His publisher, Victor Gollancz, wrote a foreword to the book, disagreeing with Orwell's condemnation of "crank" elements within the socialist movement. Nevertheless, the book's influence was far-reaching.

After a couple of months visiting the mines and back streets of the north, Orwell returned to the London area, moving a few miles north to the village of Wallington, Hertfordshire. The cottage he rented had been a small grocery shop, and he revived the business to help make ends meet while he worked on his book. He also married the first of his two wives, Eileen O'Shaughnessy, at this time.

That same year, political theory was superseded for many people by the reality of the Spanish Civil War. Not surprisingly, Orwell was drawn to this conflict between

General Francisco Franco's fascists and the various factions of communists, socialists, and anarchists. He went to Spain with the intention, he later said, of reporting for newspapers.[7] Apparently, he was so impressed by how socialist values were being implemented that he joined one of the militia groups (Partido Obrero de Unificación Marxista) and served for several months until he was wounded in the throat. His impressions of the war became the basis for his eyewitness account, *Homage to Catalonia* (1937).

Another novel, the aptly titled *Coming Up for Air*, followed as Europe stumbled into another war in 1939. Orwell was ready to enlist again, this time with British forces, but was deemed medically unfit. Instead he spent two years working as a radio producer for the British Broadcasting Corporation (BBC). In 1943, as fortunes in World War II finally shifted from Nazi Germany toward the Allies, Orwell began work on the first of the two books for which he is best known, *Animal Farm*.

THE GREAT WORKS OF HIS FINAL YEARS

For all its impact, *Animal Farm* is short and to the point, with no unnecessary description or detail. The story takes the form of a fable or allegory in which animals represent various political figures and classes in the Soviet Union. Two decades after the Russian Revolution, even some people with socialist sympathies were disillusioned by the

FABLE—*A story with a moral or purpose that uses animals in place of human characters.*

way communism had developed under Soviet dictator Joseph Stalin.

In Orwell's book, Stalin and other Soviet leaders are represented as pigs, who lead the animals in a successful revolt against the man who owns the farm. Eventually, the pigs are corrupted by power and adopt the habits and privileges of the old regime. Not only does Orwell satirize the Soviet system, he also by extension poses more universal questions about human nature and the feasibility of communism.

After tackling such weighty topics in *Animal Farm*, Orwell showed no sign of wanting to come up for air with an amusing novel, as he had after his previous works of political analysis. Perhaps personal circumstances added to his tendency toward ominous subject matter.

In 1945, Orwell's wife died in surgery, a year after the couple had adopted a son, Richard. Orwell responded by moving in 1946 to an isolated island, Jura, off the west coast of Scotland, where he wrote his last and most influential novel, *1984*.

For a man suffering from tuberculosis, Jura was probably not a good choice of residency. The wet and blustery weather did not help Orwell's medical condition or his state of mind, as he later admitted. Eventually it was too much for him, and he sought medical treatment in Glasgow and finally in London. With little time to live, he married Sonia Brownell.

Orwell used his brief postwar period to create the futuristic *1984*. It is a world in which individuality is suppressed and the state uses propaganda and surveillance to control the populace. At the head of the system is Big Brother, who is more an icon than an actual person. Orwell envisaged a future in which language itself was used to limit and shape thinking. People had to learn Newspeak, a heavily censored version of how they once spoke. In addition they were forced to accept lies through a concept called doublethink. Orwell's vision of this repressive world continues to resonate despite the fact that the year 1984 is now in the past. Modern technology has if anything increased the potential for manipulating populations in the ways *1984* describes.

DOUBLETHINK—*A term created by Orwell for* 1984 *and meaning the ability to believe two contradictory ideas at the same time.*

When Orwell died in London on January 21, 1950, he was only forty-six years old. Yet his lifetime spanned a period of immense change, both in the physical world and in people's attitudes. In Britain, the confident imperialism of the early years of the twentieth century had been shattered by two world wars and far-reaching social changes. No writer of fiction mirrored that transition more strikingly than Orwell did.

PAYING DUES

Examining *Down and Out in Paris and London*

Orwell may have wanted to be a writer from childhood, but he did not commit to this goal until he was in his mid-twenties.[1] By that time he had served in the Indian Imperial Police Force in Burma for almost five years. Meanwhile, his schoolmates had followed the conventional course of going to university at Oxford or Cambridge. He would cross paths again later with some of those who had opted for careers in writing or publishing.

Orwell had not stood out academically at Eton. Apparently university was not an option he took seriously. So, considering his family's colonial connections, the decision to travel thousands of miles to be a police officer in Burma in 1922 was not completely unexpected. Even though discipline and authority had given him trouble at school, he seemed to be ready for a life of keeping law and order in Burma.

That state of mind was not to last. Eventually, Orwell

grew disillusioned with the imperial system he was sworn to uphold, and resigned from the force while on leave in England in 1928. Illness seems to have played a part in his resignation too. He suffered from dengue fever in Burma, a condition caused by mosquito bites. Supposedly one of the consequences of this illness was depression.[2]

Orwell's police career had not been without some accomplishments. Even the training was rigorous. In addition to studying the law and police methods, he had to learn Burmese and Hindustani, adding these languages to the Greek, Latin, and French he had taken at school. At Eton, one of his French teachers was Aldous Huxley, whose own utopian classic, *Brave New World*, was published in 1932.

As an assistant superintendent, Orwell had shouldered heavy responsibilities for large areas.[3] Two of his celebrated essays from this period reflect the conflict that sometimes existed between duty and natural inclinations.

UTOPIA—*An ideal community, typically considered flawed or impractical by outsiders; derived from a sixteenth-century book written by Sir Thomas More about such a community.*

"A Hanging" details the few minutes before and after a condemned man is led to the gallows. Orwell contrasts the methodical way in which the execution is carried out with incidents and dialogue that supported his own opposition to the death penalty. The prisoner steps around a puddle to avoid getting his feet wet—a pointless act considering what he is walking toward. But it reminds us a human life is about to end. Officials, meanwhile, hover

After being born in Motihari, India, in 1903, Orwell would later serve in the Indian Imperial Police Force in Burma.

between being insensitive and wanting to get the execution over with as soon as possible.

"Shooting an Elephant" is an account in the first person of how Orwell, as the police officer responsible for a district, was called upon to deal with an escaped elephant. The animal had killed a man, but had then settled down to eat grass in a field. Orwell considers leaving the elephant alone until its owner arrives and recaptures it. But a crowd has gathered and he feels he is expected to do something decisive or he will lose face. In the end, he shoots the elephant.

Episodes like these filled Orwell with such a distaste for imperialism that, as soon as he was back in England, he made up his mind to resign from the police.[4] For a young man with a middle-class background, the decision to become a writer was a brave step met with a mixed response among his family members and acquaintances.[5] In fact, Orwell later noted that his father had been slow to accept his decision to opt for the literary life.

While in Burma, Orwell had tried to keep up with reading, and even subscribed to *Adelphi*, a left-leaning intellectual magazine that later published some of his work. But whether he had any thoughts then of writing as a career is debatable.[6] At any rate, after an extended stay with his parents at their retirement home in the coastal town of Southwold, Orwell was ready for a more serious approach to his new calling.

Naturally, the big city seemed to be the place for a young writer with ambition. A friend of his sister Marjorie found lodging for him in a cramped room on Portobello Road, in the Notting Hill district of west London. At first it was hard for him to make ends meet. For part of that first winter, a candle was his only source of heat.[7]

FIRST WORKS

As a novice, Orwell would have to learn his craft and establish a reputation. Friends later recalled laughing behind his back at his first efforts.[8] Although he was still struggling to find his voice as a writer, Orwell seemed to be certain of his subject matter. He admired the Victorian novelist Charles Dickens, who would be the subject of a later essay. Like Dickens, Orwell seemed instinctively drawn to the social issues associated with poverty and class distinctions. He began to visit London's run-down East End, dressing in old clothes and playing the tramp.[9]

Then, in the spring of 1928, he made an even more radical departure. He moved to Paris, apparently in search of literary stimulation.[10] His experiences living among some of the poorest inhabitants of the French capital were to be part of his first book, *Down and Out in Paris and London.*

Although Orwell was not the first author to examine deprivation of this kind, it still rates as a bold way to start a writing career.[11] It makes more sense, though, considering the economic and social events of the era. In 1926, Britain had witnessed a general strike, initiated by trade unions in support of miners whose wages had been cut. The strike lasted about six months, and was accompanied by much hardship and division in the country. Eventually the miners accepted the pay cut and some were left unemployed.

Orwell's comparatively well-off background meant that he had to cross the rigid social class lines of the time in order to focus attention on the conditions and injustices suffered by the poor. After working in restaurants in Paris, Orwell returned to London to await a job offer. For a month or so he lived as a tramp, staying at government institutions for the homeless or, when all else failed, sleeping outside.

At first, Orwell could not find a publisher who would accept his description of these experiences. His first version, called *A Scullion's Diary*, was finished in October 1930. After a couple of rejections, including one from poet T.S. Eliot in his capacity as an editorial director at the publisher Faber & Faber, Orwell turned his attention to writing *Burmese Days*, a novel based on his time as a colonial policeman.[12]

It was not the first rejection Orwell had faced. Attempts at a novel went nowhere.[13] Initial short stories were rejected. He did however have success with a couple of articles. "La Censure en Angleterre" [Censorship in England] was published in the French newspaper *Le Monde* [The World] on October 6, 1928. Still writing under his birth name, E.A. Blair placed "A Farthing Newspaper" in the writer G.K. Chesterton's publication, *G.K.'s Weekly*, and a piece on unemployment in the Parisian paper *Le Progrès Civique* [Civic Progress]. Both came out on December 29, 1928.[14]

What became *Down and Out in Paris and London* came close to being thrown away. Demoralized by the lack of interest in his manuscript, Orwell asked a friend, Mabel Fierz, to destroy the text but save the paper clips for future use. She was impressed with what he had written and showed it to a literary agent, Leonard Moore. He referred it to publisher Victor Gollancz.

With his left-wing sympathies, Gollancz liked Orwell's

book. He wanted some revisions and coined a new title. Orwell made the changes, and marked the acceptance of his first major work by using what would become a very famous name. He considered several pseudonyms, adopting "Orwell" from a river near Southwold.[15] Some subsequent shorter pieces of writing as well as his personal correspondence were signed by Eric Blair, but from then on his major works would be published under the name George Orwell.

DOWN AND OUT IN PARIS AND LONDON

In style, *Down and Out in Paris and London* has the flavor of a diary or a series of notes for a report. As mentioned by his biographers, however, Orwell admitted to making up or changing sequences of events to make the story flow better.[16] Names of places were also altered in some cases.

It is a stark narrative, without flowery description or even, considering the conditions, blatant emotional involvement. Certainly Orwell did not express sentimentality about the degradation he witnessed. Metaphors and similes are rare, although Orwell was capable of devising original phrases when he felt they were needed. A French woman's "dead-white face and scarlet lips," for instance, reminded him of "cold veal and tomatoes."[17] In another example, relations between kitchen staff could degenerate into "a drizzle of useless nagging, rising into storms of abuse every few minutes."[18]

DISHWASHING IN PARIS

To begin, readers are introduced to Orwell's new surroundings on his street in Paris, Rue du Coq d'Or and his lodgings at the Hotel des Trois Moineaux. Despite columns of bugs, dirt, and paper-thin walls, the hotel managed to attract a succession of poor, eccentric patrons.

No doubt it was a revelation to see how people in desperate circumstances earn their daily keep. He mentioned the Rougiers, an "old, ragged, dwarfish couple" who sold packets of postcards misrepresented as pornographic.[19] Not till they opened them later did their customers find they had paid extravagantly for pictures of local landmarks. Orwell followed up with a rambling account of Charlie, a self-absorbed Casanova who reckoned that at the age of twenty-two he was "utterly worn out and finished."[20]

Orwell spent a year and a half in the Coq d'Or district, earning a living for a time by teaching English. When even that work failed him, he resorted to pawning his clothes. Every expense had to be considered, and sometimes he was reduced to staring hungrily at food displays in shop windows. Poverty, he discovered, involved saving face in front of friends. Without work or money to occupy his time, he was often bored.

"Hunger reduces one to an utterly spineless, brainless condition," Orwell concluded.[21]

A Russian ex-soldier named Boris became his companion, and together they searched for jobs in restaurants and hotels. Needing to make a good impression on prospective employers, they had to resort to ploys such as inking skin that showed through holes in their socks.

Finally, they were offered work at a new Russian-owned restaurant called Auberge de Jehan Cottard. However, the owner was short of money, and so the opening date was constantly being pushed back. While they waited, Boris found them jobs in a hotel Orwell identified only as the "Hotel X." Orwell was hired as a *plongeur*, (a dishwasher), which he quickly discovered was the lowest position on the staff. It was an eleven-hour day at a minimum, with Sundays off if he was lucky.

Hotel staffs were categorized in a rigid hierarchy, headed by a manager and with cooks, waiters, dishwashers, and others at their respective levels. Each level had its duties and perks. To add to the complexity, employees were of many nationalities.

Dishwashers were looked down upon even by the waiters. Even so, they took pride in their work, Orwell wrote, and each wanted to be known as a *débrouillard*, a man who got the job done somehow.

Standards of hygiene and food preparation probably would have shocked the customers had they been aware, and charges for meals and rooms were geared to what it was thought a patron could afford. Orwell speculated that guests at Hotel X "were especially easy to swindle, for they were mostly Americans . . . and seemed to know nothing whatever about good food. They would stuff themselves with disgusting American 'cereals,' and eat marmalade at tea."[22]

Life for a dishwasher was a cycle of work and sleep, with a brief time for drinking, but for little else. One night Orwell heard a "fearful uproar" and, looking out of his window, saw a man lying on the street. The man had been hit on the head with a piece of lead pipe and was "quite dead."[23]

"The thing that strikes me in looking back is that I was in bed and asleep within three minutes of the murder," Orwell wrote. "So were most of the people in the street. . . . We were working people, and where was the sense of wasting sleep over a murder?"[24]

When the promised jobs at the Auberge de Jehan Cottard eventually came through, Boris and Orwell quit the Hotel X. Unfortunately, the new restaurant was still bare inside and they were expected to paint and install plumbing, among other chores, before the place could open.

After ten days of "filth and incompetence" in his new job, Orwell wrote to an acquaintance in London asking about work there. The reply, a few days later, was that there was a position open "to look after a congenital imbecile," which, Orwell remarked, "sounded a splendid rest cure" compared to his current situation.[25] He resigned and prepared to take the ferry across the English Channel.

Orwell's observations about Paris concluded with reflections about the life of a dishwasher. It was a state of slavery, he felt, allowing the worker no time to think or enjoy leisure. The higher social orders maintained such "useless drudgery," he wrote, because of a "fear of the mob." In the view of the rich, according to this theory, if workers had leisure time they would be dangerous: "The educated man pictures a horde of submen, wanting only a day's liberty to loot his house, burn his books, and set him to work minding a machine or sweeping out a lavatory."[26]

In fact, Orwell argued, the mob was already loose "and—in the shape of rich men—is using its power to set up enormous treadmills of boredom, such as 'smart' hotels."[27]

ON THE STREETS OF LONDON

Arriving in London, Orwell found that yet another job offer had been put on hold. He had a month to kill. With a loan to tide him over, he acquainted himself with London's version of being down and out.

His account of London differed from that of Paris, with the focus this time more on lodging and lifestyle than on the workplace. With the prospect of a job in the near future, Orwell was more occupied with profiling his fellow indigents.

One similarity with Paris, however, was the reliance on pawnbrokers to acquire money for living expenses. After visiting one such place, Orwell was able to pay rent by exchanging a decent suit for some cash and ragged clothes. Putting on the latter, he found, changed people's attitudes toward him. "When a badly dressed man passes them they shudder away," he wrote.[28]

With time to contemplate, Orwell considered the differences between London and Paris. London, he decided, was "cleaner and quieter and drearier. . . . The crowds were better dressed and the faces comelier and milder and more alike, without that fierce individuality and malice of the French. There was less drunkenness, and less dirt, and less quarrelling, and more idling."[29]

In addition to the private lodging houses in which Orwell and other itinerants stayed, England had a network of government workhouses commonly known as "spikes" and "casual wards." These provided overnight shelter for "a graceless, mangy crew" of ragged, underfed tramps, unemployed factory hands and farm workers, and others down on their luck.[30] Conditions were spartan and discipline was strict. Rations usually were limited to bread, margarine, and tea or sugarless cocoa. Men often slept on the floor, with a single tub of water for everyone's washing needs.

As Boris had been Orwell's friend in Paris, so Paddy, an Irishman in his mid-thirties, became his companion in London. "He had two subjects of conversation, the shame and come-down of being a tramp, and the best way of getting a free meal," Orwell wrote, adding, "He had the regular character of a tramp—abject, envious, a jackal's character."[31]

Orwell also befriended Bozo, a pavement artist or, to use the slang term for the trade, a screever. A talented artist, Bozo spent his days painting scenes and cartoons on the sidewalk for tips from passersby. Each day he had to start afresh, having cleaned his work off the pavement when he finished the previous day.

In line with Orwell's own philosophy, Bozo was an atheist. He was the sort "who does not so much disbelieve in God as personally dislike him."[32] Despite a general pessimism about the human condition, though, Bozo felt education could help a man rise above poverty.

While some London beggars had genuine talents, such as Bozo's, others had to resort to less respectable work. Street photographers, acrobats, organ grinders, match sellers, and street singers were among these, in Orwell's view. All the same, Orwell did not consider them parasites. What they did to make money was no less useful and honest than what was done by many others, he argued. What set beggars apart was their failure to earn a decent living. "Money has become the grand test of virtue," he concluded.[33]

With his month-long wait for work almost over, Orwell was ready to wind up his time on the road. He ended his book by considering why men become tramps. One reason, he felt, was English anti-vagrancy laws, which kept people moving from place to place in order to find overnight shelter so that they had no opportunity to settle anywhere. The three main evils in a tramp's life, he wrote, were hunger, enforced idleness, and lack of contact with women, which he felt made transients feel degraded and demoralized.[34]

Orwell suggested establishing small farms to provide work for the tramps. That would make them feel useful and give them a reason to stay in one place. It would be better than the accommodations available for a homeless person, as described by Orwell. They ranged from Salvation Army hostels, which Orwell disliked because their "numerous restrictions stink of prison and charity," to park benches and wooden boxes.[35]

Despite feeling that he had not seen "more than the fringe of poverty," Orwell thought he had learned "one or two things" from his wanderings. First, he would never again consider all tramps to be "drunken scoundrels." Not surprisingly, after what he had seen in Parisian kitchens, he was also wary of eating in "smart restaurants."[36]

REFLECTIONS ON BURMA

Examining *Burmese Days, A Clergyman's Daughter,* **and** *Keep the Aspidistra Flying*

Early in the 1930s Orwell was working on two books at once. He was still making changes to *Down and Out in Paris and London* while he was writing *Burmese Days*. Despite the overlap, the two books are very different.

Down and Out reads as if it came directly from Orwell's own experiences. The few changes he made in the real sequence of events are not acknowledged in the text, although Orwell's comments made to friends and annotations in a copy of the book are revealing.[1] The most obvious shortcoming of the book, Orwell conceded, was the pairing of two dissimilar episodes—dishwashing in Paris and tramping in southern England. They both focus on poverty, but the circumstances, as some critics have noted, are not comparable.[2]

One alteration that stands out concerns the job offer that, as Orwell wrote it, brought him back to London from Paris. After his return, he did tutor a local boy for a time while he was alternating between his parents' home in Southwold and his tramping. It appears this was the "congenital imbecile" to whom he referred in his text. But this position had nothing to do with his return from Paris.[3] The real reason was that, one of his biographers noted, the magazine *Adelphi* accepted an article by him about tramps.[4]

Response to *Down and Out* was favorable for the most part.[5] A notable exception was a letter to *The Times* newspaper of London from a restaurateur complaining that Orwell's descriptions of dirty hotel conditions had brought the catering business into disrepute. As might be expected, Orwell felt compelled to reply with a letter of his own.[6]

Nevertheless, Orwell continued with *Burmese Days*, confident that it would be published. Success as a writer did not guarantee financial stability, however. In April 1932, lack of income forced him to take a job as a teacher in a small private school near London. Typically, he did not waste the experience. It was to show up later as the basis for part of his second novel, *A Clergyman's Daughter.*

BURMESE DAYS

In his first novel, *Burmese Days*, Orwell had more freedom to adapt and reshape his memories than *Down and Out* had allowed. While his observations about Paris and London were constrained somewhat by the eyewitness format, *Burmese Days* was conceived as a work of fiction. As such, it incorporates the flowing plot, character development, and evocative descriptions of places one would expect from a work guided by the imagination.

What the two books do have in common, at first glance, is their setting in exotic locations in which Orwell had lived. Even the rough areas of London described in *Down and Out* would have been unfamiliar to many of Orwell's middle-class readers. More important, they both embody Orwell's emerging concern about injustice and inequality within the British class system and, by extension, in the colonies. In addition, both show flashes of the satire and irony he would develop so effectively in his later works.

Burmese Days is set in the mid-1920s, during the last years of Britain's imperial domination of the region. Burma, now called Myanmar, was administered by Britain as part of India. As reflected in Orwell's writing, British colonial residents were becoming less confident in their imperial role. There is not the enthusiasm so evident in the literature of a decade or two earlier. Back then, Rudyard Kipling set the standard with a torrent of patriotic stories and poems, such as *Kim* and *The Jungle Book*.

Like another novel of the period, E.M. Forster's classic, *A Passage To India*, *Burmese Days* is about the seemingly unbridgeable gulf between races, between the ruled and the rulers. In contrast to the gung ho attitudes portrayed in the stories of an earlier era, Orwell clearly regarded the colonial administration as corrupt. In *Burmese Days*, the British conspire to keep their status as a privileged ruling caste, and the more educated and ambitious among the Burmese and Indians struggle to emulate their rulers.

Characters in *Burmese Days* are almost invariably self-centered and conniving, bending principle to further their own interests. In the case of the British, the aim is to keep the Burmese in a subservient role and to remain as detached from them as possible. The Burmese can scheme too. The opening chapter introduces a minor official, U Po Kyin, who sets out to manipulate British and Burmese alike for his own advantage. The absurdities and contradictions in such a society are ripe for satire, and Orwell obliges with a great eye for detail. In one celebrated passage, two British officials disagree about who has the right to kick a servant.

Orwell also shows an inclination to play upon the physical attributes of his characters to emphasize aspects of his plots. It was something he would repeat in subsequent novels—for example, detailing George Bowling's aging in *Coming Up for Air* in such a way as to anticipate changing times in the story as a whole. Kyin, in this case, is described as a man who was overweight and proud of his excesses.

Much of Orwell's viewpoint is expressed through his main character, John Flory, a timber merchant in his mid-thirties. An indication of Orwell's identification with his protagonist comes from an early version of the story, written in the first person with Flory as narrator.[7] To what extent Orwell held Flory's anti-colonial views while he was still in Burma is questionable. One biographer assumes that Orwell's distaste toward colonialism developed gradually. As a man who valued his privacy, he often had mixed feelings and probably did not share them readily.[8] For one thing, police discipline would not have allowed him to speak out.

Typical of the other British expatriates, Flory divides his time between his house with servants, the whites-only club, and lengthy working trips into the jungle surrounding the small, isolated community where they live. Unlike his fellow countrymen, however, Flory associates with the native people of the region and shows an interest in local customs and plant life. He even makes friends with a physician from India, Dr. Veraswami, which earns him the disapproval of his peers.

Flory is self-conscious about a birthmark on his face, and this is reinforced by the arrival of a beautiful young woman from England, Elizabeth Lackersteen. After years of isolation Flory is attracted to this like-minded companion and she is prodded toward matrimony by her matchmaking aunt.

Orwell makes it clear that there are profound incompatibilities between the intended couple. The shallow and superior Elizabeth Lackersteen is inclined toward the racism that John Flory disdains in his fellow administrators. She instinctively adopts all the prejudices and dislikes of the expatriates. Even so, Flory is devastated when a young military police officer, Verrall, arrives on temporary assignment and sweeps Elizabeth off her feet.

Elizabeth's fickle aunt encourages the new attachment, impressed by Verrall's aristocratic family pedigree.

Forming a subplot is U Po Kyin's sly plan to defeat Dr. Veraswami, his rival for British approval. Important consequences stem from this rivalry. But the focus of the story is always on Flory and his attempt to deal with the inadequacies and yearnings that give dimension to his character.

His birthmark seems to be a manifestation of this inner turmoil, which contrasts with Verrall's relatively brief appearance in the story. Indeed, the differences between the two characters are striking. Verrall seems almost a caricature. He is rugged, confident, shows little or no emotion, and has minimal regard for others. Add his noble background and he is a magnet for eligible young women. In contrast, Flory's emotional commitments, notably his infatuation with Elizabeth, lead him to disaster.

Considering *Burmese Days* was a first novel, it is a promising study of individual character and the politics and social climate of the time. Orwell drew from his own understanding of exile in the service of empire, and was not slow to state his conclusions. The empire was a despotism, he proclaimed, "benevolent, no doubt, but still a despotism with theft as its final object."As such, it was "a stifling, stultifying world" both for the rulers and ruled.[9]

Orwell even worked identifiable episodes from his own life into the story. He briefly mentioned the celebrated tale about the shooting of an elephant, which was to appear in essay form in 1936. As so often in Orwell's work, individuals in this anecdote, described in detail in the essay, tailor their behavior and actions to meet with the expectations of the crowd.

Burmese Days was completed while Orwell was still teaching. He had little free time; virtually his only other pursuit was enjoying the outdoors. All his life he enjoyed nature, and during this period he found an outlet by planting a vegetable garden.

Late in 1933, his love of the outdoors had an unfortunate consequence. During a rainy motorcycle ride, Orwell was unprepared for the weather and possibly as a result contracted a life-threatening bout of pneumonia requiring a short hospital stay.[10]

Prospects for his novel were not immediately promising. *Down and Out in Paris and London* had not sold well despite critical praise. Besides, publisher Victor Gollancz was hesitant to publish *Burmese Days* for reasons unrelated to potential sales. He feared that some portrayals in the novel were close enough to real characters to risk libel actions. He was also afraid the government would try to prevent publication of a book so unsympathetic toward colonialism. It took an American publisher, Harper Brothers, to accept the manuscript before Gollancz would agree to a British edition in June 1935.[11] As it turned out, Gollancz's fears were unfounded.

A NEW PROJECT

Pressure on the individual to conform to social or political conventions continues as an Orwellian theme with his next novel, *A Clergyman's Daughter.* This time the protagonist is Dorothy Hare, the daughter of a church minister in a country parish in eastern England, not far from London.

The inspiration for the title was Brenda Salkeld, a friend Orwell had met in Southwold and who happened to be a clergyman's daughter. However, little else of Brenda went into Dorothy and her adventures.[12] In contrast with the naiveté of the fictional daughter, Brenda apparently shared some of Orwell's intellectual and literary interests.[13]

Not for the first time in Orwell's friendships with females, the relationship with Brenda did not develop romantically.[14] This certainly appears to have been the case too with his old friend, Jacintha Buddicom. As a teenager he had written poems to her inviting a more intimate union, but she was not receptive. She even asked him to change a suggestive word in one poem, entitled "The Pagan." Orwell obliged, substituting "unarmoured souls" for "naked souls."[15]

Biographers speculate about Orwell's relations with women during his time in Burma. John Flory, in Orwell's novel, had a Burmese mistress whom he treated rather badly. Whether Orwell had such a formal arrangement is not known, but it would be consistent with colonial practices. As far as his work is concerned, the most direct evidence is poems that survive from this period about encounters with prostitutes.[16]

He had a closer relationship with another Southwold friend, Eleanor Jaques, during the time he was writing

A Clergyman's Daughter. Aspects of their friendship appear in his subsequent novel, *Keep the Aspidistra Flying*. In particular, Orwell drew from a country walk they took—mining the same material much later for a scene in *1984*.[17] From most accounts though, not until Orwell met his future wife Eileen O'Shaughnessy at a London party did he find a suitable marriage prospect.

A CLERGYMAN'S DAUGHTER

Reviewers wrote favorably about *A Clergyman's Daughter*.[18] Biographers have been less kind about Orwell's construction of the lead character—"a muddle," according to one—and even the author himself did not rate the book very highly in later years.[19]

Dorothy lives in a world cramped by petty restrictions. Like John Flory in *Burmese Days*, she is weighed down by the routine and conformity of a small, insular community and afraid of going against other people's expectations of correct behavior. In Dorothy's case, the pressure is arguably worse. Though she does not have to endure homesickness, like the expatriate Flory, she is instead little short of a slave to her father's whims and the needs of the parish. When she is exposed to worldly experiences, she struggles to retain her faith and religion. Orwell sometimes wrote as if belief in God was a thing of the past, and he used the opportunity here to poke fun at religious practices.

Orwell's confidence as a writer was on the increase, judging by this witty satire. He was particularly scathing about what he clearly regarded as the petty distinctions of English religious life. Not only were there differences between various denominations, between the Church of England (the Anglicans) and Roman Catholics and Nonconformists such as Methodists and Baptists, but also there was disagreement within the Anglican religion itself.

In Dorothy's home parish, for example, the church schoolmaster, Victor Stone, wants more ceremony, more use of incense and choirs, in the services. Dorothy's father, the Reverend Charles Hare, on the other hand, is strongly opposed to that, and even dislikes the ritual involved in annual church events like the harvest festival. The Rev. Hare's attitude turns off many people in his parish, and as a result his congregation has shrunk.

At first, Dorothy seems to be accepting her way of life without much questioning. She may worry about her father's unpaid housekeeping bills and all the things she has to do for the parish, but her sense of purpose, or duty, is strong. As the central character of the story, Dorothy seems to be set up for a fall. Something has to give in her frazzled life for the plot to progress. The trigger for this is the introduction by Orwell of the roguish middle-aged Mr. Warburton.

An artist and atheist with a shady love life, Warburton is disapproved of by the town's more conventional residents, most notably by his next-door neighbor, the gossipy

Mrs. Semprill. He in turn disapproves of many of them, and plays devil's advocate by teasing Dorothy about her religious faith and by trying to seduce her. Despite her rejection of his opinions and behavior, Dorothy evidently likes Warburton. He is good-humored, after all, and not judgmental and stern like her father. Inevitably, the relationship—innocent as it is on her part—leads to trouble.

As in *Burmese Days*, Orwell kept his style and vocabulary simple and avoided flowery description. He used metaphors and similes frugally, but when he did they tend to be memorable. For example, he described a face "as pale as a silver coin," recycling an image he had used to describe the moon in *Burmese Days*.[20]

He was no less effective than in his previous novel in making observations about individual people as well as the community as a whole. His political leanings toward the left are apparent sometimes. A remark about living in the past being a luxury for those who can afford it hints at his agreement with that socialist insult, "the idle rich."[21]

Orwell also went into detail, and showed he knew what he was talking about, in describing the working life of the lower rungs of society. One section of the book is set in the hop fields of the county of Kent, where the London poor, the homeless, and gypsies make up a migrant summer workforce that picks the hops used to make beer. Another section is set in a private girls' school, which the owner ruthlessly runs to extract maximum profit from the fee-paying parents.

Perhaps the major shortcoming in *A Clergyman's Daughter* is a rather clumsy plot development and a tendency toward caricature.[22] The plot hinges on Dorothy's lapse, and then recovery, of memory. This is perhaps a bit too convenient to be entirely believable. The same could be said of the character portraits, which fit well into parody only because Orwell has pared them down to figures of fun. But, then again, that is part of the appeal of the story.

Orwell was in an experimental frame of mind at times while writing this book. Chapter Three begins with a lengthy exchange of quirky, rather nonsensical, conversation—written in the form of a theatrical play—between various individuals, mostly down and outs, in London's Trafalgar Square. Like so many writers before and since, Orwell was clearly influenced by James Joyce's groundbreaking 1922 novel, *Ulysses*.

During this dialogue, incidentally, one of the characters sings lyrics beginning with the words "Keep the aspidistra flying," which would become the title of Orwell's next book. The phrase suggests the idea of patriotically flying a flag. The aspidistra, a large-leafed houseplant that was a favorite in middle-class English homes, is used as a symbol of common values. This was one chapter that was not well-received by critics.[23]

In his major work, at least, Orwell never repeated such experimentation. Realizing perhaps that his talents veered more toward documentary than fantasy, he attempted to become more lucid and precise in his writing. He was his own worst critic, and he did not hesitate to express his opinions about the writings of others. Even works by friends such as Arthur Koestler and Anthony Powell received adverse criticism, both in book reviews and in person, when Orwell thought it appropriate.

KEEP THE ASPIDISTRA FLYING

In his third novel, *Keep the Aspidistra Flying*, Orwell continued to focus on the way a person is conditioned and restrained by social pressures. Most of the central characters in his novels struggle with the expectations of the communities in which they live.

In *Burmese Days*, John Flory resents the narrow-minded attitudes of colonial society and rebels against them in a limited way. Dorothy Hare, the clergyman's daughter, is virtually a slave to the demands of her father and his parish. Gordon Comstock, the 29-year-old Londoner at the center of *Keep the Aspidistra Flying*, is no less preoccupied with conventions. Unlike the other two, though, he wastes no time in rejecting them.

When Orwell introduces him, Gordon is working in a London bookshop, just as Orwell once did. In October 1934, less than a month after finishing *A Clergyman's Daughter*, Orwell left his parents' home in Southwold yet again, this time for a new job and new lodgings in the north London borough of Hampstead. The new novel was to draw extensively from these surroundings and the people he met there.

The protagonist, Gordon Comstock, considers his sales position in a bookshop a dead-end job. But it does provide the money to rent a room—a bed-sitter—in a house divided into similar accommodations. His landlady, Mrs. Wisbeach, provides dinner, which Gordon supplements by secretly making cups of tea in his room, heating the water with an oil lamp. This and occasional letters from his girl-friend, Rosemary, are about his only pleasures. Making tea and visits from women friends are of course strictly forbidden by Mrs. Wisbeach.

Gordon is in rebellion against money. He hates the way wealth dictates the choices people can make in their lives. He cannot even afford to go out to a pub for a drink with his fellow lodger, whom he knows simply by his last name, Flaxman. Allowing Flaxman to buy him a drink would be an unacceptable act of charity in Gordon's view. He would rather go without.

Lack of money compromises his other relationships too. On his infrequent outings with Rosemary, Gordon is tortured by his inability to pay for things and yet he refuses to accept the indignity of letting her pay her own way. For this theme, Orwell apparently drew from his own misgivings when he was going out with Eleanor Jaques.

Gordon's other main friend is Ravelston, a wealthy man with socialist political views. Ravelston is the editor of *Antichrist*, a magazine to which Gordon sometimes contributes his poetry. The friendship is strained by the contrast between their financial situations. Once again, Gordon shuns Ravelston's offer of money. Ravelston, for his part, is often embarrassed because his wealth and upper-class background do not fit well with socialism or the people he meets through his magazine.

Ravelston's girlfriend, Hermione, does not help with his dilemma. She is bored by socialism, has never read *Antichrist*, and complains that the "lower classes" smell.[24] Ravelston still adores her and, as always, avoids disagreement.

Life has not always been this bleak for Gordon. He used to have a good, well-paying job writing advertising copy. The company he worked for, New Albion, had contracts to publicize various products. With his background as an aspiring poet and his way with words, Gordon could expect to do well in this career.

However, success in the world of capitalism is the last thing Gordon wants. Not only is it contrary to his politics but it is hard for him to accept culturally. He comes from a family that in generations past enjoyed a higher social status. Commerce is still a little beneath people with his background. The description could have fit Orwell's family, the Blairs, just as easily.

Orwell describes the Comstocks as "middle middle class, the landless gentry." They are "one of those families which rose on the wave of Victorian prosperity and then sank again."[25]

In addition, Gordon has a typical young man's dread

of being tied down by a job and of one day having a family and a home to support.

In developing this story, Orwell was once again tackling themes that were particularly applicable to the English. The perception of the English as being slow to show their feelings and willing to tolerate bad conditions rather than complain may be a little dated, but it has relevance to Orwell's portrayals. Success involves too many compromises of Gordon's character and ethics. Even his small triumphs as a poet he tends to shrug off rather than acknowledge with any satisfaction.

Gordon's self-esteem is so low that when he is invited to a party and arrives at the address to find no one there he assumes he is the victim of a trick rather than accepting the more logical explanation that he got the date wrong.

Overall, then, Gordon can be said to be a product of his class, nationality, and era. His misery is largely self-inflicted. He could have made more money if he had kept his job as a copywriter, but he rejected that lifestyle and the values that went with it. He invites suffering as if it were a penance. Poverty and the consequent loneliness and deprivation are the price of keeping his soul.

Having devised Gordon's outlook on life, Orwell continues his novel almost as if he were conducting a social experiment. What happens, he seems to be asking, when someone tries to live without regard for money? Gordon is the guinea pig who finds out.

Lack of money becomes more and more of an obstacle

for Gordon. When he takes Rosemary for a day in the country, he runs out of money and has to borrow from her. She is happy to pay her own way, but the shame of it is enough to spoil the romance he had anticipated. As he explains to her, "one doesn't *feel* a human being—unless one's got money in one's pocket."[26]

As is often the case with human nature, the pendulum swings from deprivation into excess. One of Gordon's poems is accepted by an American publication, and he is paid the then-substantial sum of ten pounds. His immediate thought is to give half of it to his long-suffering sister Julia, from whom he frequently borrows money without repaying it. Instead he invites Rosemary and Ravelston for an extravagant meal at a restaurant and gets drunk. Rosemary walks off after tiring of Gordon's rowdy behavior. He then hires a couple of prostitutes, dragging along the reluctant Ravelston.

The next morning Gordon wakes up in a police cell, charged with being drunk and disorderly. His job and lodgings are lost once the news of his arrest appears in the local newspaper. Fortunately, Ravelston sticks by him. And so, for that matter, does Rosemary. If anyone can change him, she can. Social conventions and the need to make money are linked to human nature after all, it seems.

Orwell kept his style as direct and simple as it had been in his previous work. His strong opinions about social and political issues are woven into virtually every page. Perhaps he was a little too opinionated. At times he piled up generalizations about people with an enthusiasm that might seem excessive. In describing his characters, particularly in the early pages, he often wrote about them as "the sort" or "type" of people that act or look a certain way. Julia, for instance, is "one of those girls who even at their most youthful remind one irresistibly of a goose."[27]

Orwell's language is descriptive but not especially original in this novel. "Motheaten" is an adjective that he used repeatedly in depicting Gordon's run-down state. Every once in a while, though, Orwell had a fresh way of viewing things. A London tram becomes, through Gordon's eyes, "a raucous swan of steel."[28]

Some of Orwell's references may not be easily understood by today's readers. Gordon obsesses over a coin, commonly known as a joey in Orwell's day and now long out of circulation in Britain. He dreads being "a soldier in the strap-hanging army," the straps in question being what commuters on the London Underground trains hung onto to keep their balance.[29] (New York subway riders today are still nicknamed "straphangers.")

Orwell's observations about class and politics were acute. The rigid divisions between people of different classes in Britain form an important theme throughout Orwell's work. Despite his socialist sympathies, though, he did not glorify or whitewash any particular segment of the population.

In fact, Orwell could be scathing about individuals from all backgrounds, including Gordon himself. People's cultural and artistic tastes were a recurring target.

Gordon's customers at the bookshop are ridiculed: a "lower-class woman, looking like a draggled duck nosing among garbage" and "a plump little sparrow of a woman, red-cheeked, middle-middle class, carrying under her arm a copy of *The Forsyte Saga*—title outwards, so that passers-by could spot her for a highbrow."[30]

Gordon's interest in writing also allowed Orwell to comment on his contemporaries and immediate predecessors in the profession. Most of them Gordon considers to be "dud stuff" and "damp squibs." Gordon is even more negative about the movies, which he regards as a drug for friendless people. Passing a theater displaying photographs of actress Greta Garbo, starring in *The Painted Veil* (based on a novel by Somerset Maugham), Gordon says to himself: "Why encourage the art that is destined to replace literature?"[31]

ORWELL'S FUTURE WIFE

Keep the Aspidistra Flying is considered to be closer to Orwell's own life than his other fiction.[32] But it did not include allusions to two incidents from this period that were to become integral parts of Orwell's biographical background.

Years after Orwell's death, fellow writer Rayner Heppenstall published an account alleging that Orwell had struck him with a stick while the two were sharing an apartment in the latter part of 1935. Orwell, Heppenstall suggested, had been a sadist. Another source countered that Heppenstall had been drinking and behaving badly and perhaps deserved to be hit. Whatever the truth, the two men made up their differences, but Orwell never recorded his side of the story.[33]

Far more important at this time was the first meeting between Orwell and Eileen O'Shaughnessy, who was to become his wife. They met at a party through an old school friend of Orwell, the writer Cyril Connolly. Orwell remarked after the party that Eileen was "the sort of girl I would like to marry."[34]

A graduate of Oxford University, where she had studied English, Eileen was working on a master's degree in psychology at University College London. Orwell, it seems, was attracted by her intelligence and humor. Also, her socialist politics found common ground with his own opinions. By the time Orwell completed *Keep the Aspidistra Flying*, they had already talked about marriage.

SETTING COURSE FOR WIGAN

Examining *The Road to Wigan Pier*

With *Keep the Aspidistra Flying* finished, Orwell was relieved to be moving on. As usual, there would be requests from the publisher for changes to his manuscript, in large part to guard against libel suits.[1] But, other than that, he was free to take on something new.

Biographers differ slightly about what prompted Orwell to embark on his next book. Apparently there was no proposal for another novel. Instead, it was suggested that he should write about working conditions and poverty in northern England. Whether this suggestion came from a newspaper editor[2] or his publisher Victor Gollancz [3] has been subject to question, as has Gollancz's support for the project. There is even doubt about Orwell's motives. Was he doing it for the money, so that he could afford to marry Eileen? According to one biographer, Orwell said much later that he was "rather ashamed" of

The Road to Wigan Pier and wanted it to be suppressed along with some of his earlier books.[4]

At any rate, at the end of January 1936, Orwell took a train north from London, and made his way from one city to another, settling on Wigan as the heart of his study. *The Road to Wigan Pier* can be seen as a turning point for Orwell both as a writer and a political thinker. What he witnessed made a deep impression,[5] and pushed him toward a simpler and more focused literary style and a deeper commitment to politics. It also put him in the public eye to an extent his novels had not.

As a work of nonfiction about a particular era in English social and political history, *Road* requires a patient reader. References to circumstances in the Europe of the early twentieth century may seem obscure today. The English class system of that era appears outmoded and much has changed in the decades since.

In Orwell's time, however, class distinctions were the foundation of a rigid hierarchy. Workers and the middle and upper classes were segregated by economic interests and everyday lifestyles. The gulf between classes was such that meaningful contact was limited and there was widespread ignorance and prejudice toward one another.

Adding to these tensions was the rise of fascism, with its emphasis on a disciplined, nationalistic society. In the mid-1930s, when Orwell first published, fascist parties had control of Italy, under Mussolini, and Germany, under Hitler. Several other countries, including Britain, had fascist movements that conceivably could have been a threat to the established order. Orwell and many of his contemporaries saw Europe facing a critical showdown between fascism and socialism.

Orwell was attracted by the ideals of socialism, which included public ownership of property, collective effort and classless equality. Socialism had several different adherents. There were those who believed that change had to be violently imposed and rigidly upheld, like the communist regime in Russia, as well as supporters of democratic methods of reform.

Orwell never leaves much doubt about his support for democracy. He used *The Road to Wigan Pier* as a platform for urging people of the lower and middle classes to put aside their differences and close ranks against fascism. The first part of the book is devoted to describing some of the hardships and injustices suffered by the working classes, in particular the miners of northwest England.

ORWELL'S ROAD TO SOCIALISM

About halfway through *The Road to Wigan Pier*, Orwell switched to his own background. As a teenage schoolboy he describes himself as a socialist without having a clear idea of what that meant. Like many young people in the years immediately after World War I ended in 1918, however, he was in "a revolutionary mood."[6] The slaughter of the war, he felt, was the fault of incompetent old men who should be thrown out of power.

"By 1918," he wrote, "everyone under forty was in a bad temper with his elders, and the mood of anti-militarism which followed naturally upon the fighting was extended into a general revolt against orthodoxy and authority."[7]

In his early twenties, of course, he was trying to uphold that authority as a police officer in Burma. That experience turned him into an opponent of British imperialism and, by implication, imperialism in general. The tone and themes were set for much of his subsequent work. His first novel, *Burmese Days*, clearly drew from his time as a colonial official. It is not so obvious, until reading Orwell's explanation, that *Down and Out in Paris and London* also stemmed from his time in Burma. He regarded both the Burmese and the English working classes as victims of injustice, he wrote in *The Road to Wigan Pier*. The Burmese were oppressed by colonialism and the workers by capitalism.

"I felt that I [had] to escape," he continued, "not merely from imperialism but from every form of man's dominion over man. I wanted to submerge myself, to get right down among the oppressed, to be one of them and on their side against their tyrants. . . . At that time failure seemed to me to be the only virtue. Every suspicion of self-advancement, even to 'succeed' in life to the extent of making a few hundreds a year, seemed to me spiritually ugly, a species of bullying."[8]

These thoughts show the motivation for Orwell's personal odysseys into the lives of the homeless and the poor.

The same ideas are also reflected in the plots of *A Clergyman's Daughter* and *Keep the Aspidistra Flying*. They are also evident in his decision to fight for socialism in Spain. Ultimately, Orwell's pursuit of their implications led to his landmark works, *Animal Farm* and *1984*.

After explaining his personal background, Orwell went on in *Road* to discuss socialism as a solution to social problems. Other than describing socialist doctrine as "elementary common sense" with liberty and justice at its heart, he did not elaborate much about its theories.[9] He was far more concerned with the practical challenge of winning converts. For socialism to take its deserved place as the best way of tackling social and political challenges, it had to solve its image problem. Many ordinary people were not interested in socialism because they disliked its proponents. Too many socialists, Orwell wrote, were petty intellectuals who indulge in obscure ideological arguments. Socialists were also represented by various types of off-putting cranks, Orwell wrote, including feminists and vegetarians.

Even the literature associated with British socialism was "dull, tasteless, and bad," Orwell added. Typically, he was not afraid to name writers he thought fit this description. About the best of them, he felt, was the poet W.H. Auden, "a sort of gutless Kipling." However, he later apologized for that "spiteful remark."[10]

In addition to being on sale to the public, *Road* had also been chosen as a selection for subscribers to the Left Book Club. Organized by Victor Gollancz, the club promoted a book a month reflecting reformist and anti-fascist views. That the club hierarchy would choose a book as scathing about people within the socialist movement must have come as a shock to some readers. Orwell's critique of British socialism was controversial among influential members of that movement.

When the book was first published in 1937, it included a foreword by Gollancz, addressing the controversy. To summarize, Gollancz pointed out that the club tried to reflect diverse views from the political left. It did not try to censor or gag its authors.

Personally, Gollancz concluded, he disagreed with Orwell on a number of issues. Orwell, he felt, still retained some of the prejudices of his class on such topics as pacifism, feminism, and vegetarianism. Overall, though, he praised the book for showing the need to "rouse the apathetic" and to "equip ourselves by thought and study" to lead people into socialism once they had been roused.[11]

Among many of his readers and literary peers, however, Orwell was widely praised for his description of the working life of a miner. Apparently Orwell's observations did not please all of Wigan's residents. In his book *Peering at Wigan*, published in the early 1990s and now out of print, local journalist Geoffrey Shryhane wrote that "most educated locals" wished he had gone elsewhere to do his research. He had sought out "the worst side of Wigan life."[12] That might have suited his purpose in terms of illustrating the extremes of poverty. But, as a mining official quoted by Shryhane observed, Orwell "could have chosen to go to one of a thousand respectable working class houses" instead of the filthy, run-down lodging he ended up with—in which case he would have left Wigan with very different impressions.[13]

IMPRESSIONS OF WIGAN

Evidently Orwell started his research on *Road* without knowing quite what to expect. He visited several cities before settling on the town of Wigan. Closures of cotton mills and mines had put many people there out of work. Orwell arrived by train in early February 1936 and found a place to stay at a house that doubled as a shop selling tripe. The stomach lining of a cow, tripe was a common ingredient in the local diet.

An ex-miner, Mr. Brooker, and his wife were the tenants of the house, and Orwell began his account by describing the other lodgers and the conditions under which they lived. Dirt, dust, grime, and grease permeated Orwell's impressions. Names, of course, were often changed so that the people he wrote about were not easily identifiable.

Of Mr. Brooker he wrote that "like all people with permanently dirty hands he had a peculiarly intimate, lingering manner of handling things. If he gave you a slice of bread-and-butter there was always a black thumb-print on it."[14]

In its grimness, the landscape throughout the industrial areas seemed like an extension of the Brookers' home. Smoke from factory chimneys and slag heaps from the mines are the kind of images that dominate. For many of his contemporaries, especially those of the middle and upper classes in the more pastoral south of the country, places like Wigan were as far outside their experience as a foreign land. They might well have thought, as Orwell clearly imagined they did, that the working class was too ignorant to experience suffering and too lazy to work if it could be avoided.

To counter those views, Orwell wrote of a train journey during which he caught a fleeting glimpse of a woman trying to unblock a drainpipe at the back of her row house. She had "the usual exhausted face of the slum girl who is twenty-five and looks forty, thanks to miscarriages and drudgery; and it wore, for the second in which I saw it, the most desolate, hopeless expression I have ever seen." That woman knew well enough, Orwell wrote, "how dreadful a destiny it was" to be in her situation.[15]

To his credit, Orwell made a consistent effort to base his book on direct observation rather than on secondhand impressions. Although he could not see everything during his brief time in Wigan, he tried to meet people and to sample their lives. He found irony in the fact that workers who were so important to the country's economy lived such miserable lives. Western civilization was founded on coal, he pointed out. At that time, it was the principal energy source for electricity, machinery, and transportation, not to mention heating. "In the metabolism of the

Western world," Orwell noted, "the coal-miner is second in importance only to the man who ploughs the soil."[16]

A visit to a mine called Cribben's Pit was arranged by Orwell's initial contact in Wigan, Jerry Kennan, who worked in the town's electricity department. The tall Orwell promptly banged his head on a girder on the way down to the coal face and passed out, according to Shryhane's account. He revived and continued his tour, but was exhausted by the time he emerged back at the top.

At six feet two and a half inches, Orwell must have been an ungainly giant next to the mostly shorter miners. Once they exited the cage—the rudimentary elevator that descended into the mine to the level where the coal was being worked—they sometimes had to walk for miles through tunnels to the area where the seam was being worked. The tunnels were so low that the miners could only walk stooped over.

The coal face itself, Orwell estimated, was three or four feet high. This meant that the "fillers," the men who shoveled the coal from the face to a conveyor belt running behind them, had to work on their knees. Heat, dust, and the noise of the conveyor belt added to their discomfort. Cave-ins and gas explosions were their deadliest hazards. The coal had to be blasted loose. A miscalculation in the size of the charge could cause injury and death.

Even the cage could be the source of accidents if the operator let it descend too fast or the cable to which it was attached snapped. Orwell reported that "there have been cases of the cage crashing into the pit-bottom at its very maximum speed." With the men inside knowing seconds ahead that they were doomed, Orwell speculated that it would be "a dreadful way to die."[17]

After considering miners' low wages and inadequate pensions, Orwell turned his attention to housing. Local government authorities were replacing some of the slums with areas of public housing known as "estates." Even though this was an improvement, Orwell conceded, it came with a social cost. In relocating from their old derelict neighborhoods, tenants lost their sense of community. These housing projects were usually built on the outskirts of the towns, and Orwell's research found that they seemed remote and unfriendly to many of their new residents. They no longer had access to familiar shops and pubs, which in any case were probably demolished along with the slums. In addition, the estates had restrictions on keeping pigeons, a messy but popular hobby among the miners.

UNEMPLOYMENT AND THE FUTURE

Unemployment in Britain was around two million at the time Orwell was writing *Road*. But official statistics did not take into account dependent family members, Orwell wrote, so that a much greater number was directly affected by the resulting poverty and malnutrition.

An unemployed person had to declare any sources of

income before qualifying for government assistance. This was called the means test. If an elderly parent was living in the family home, the parent's pension could be enough for disqualification. Orwell wrote that he knew of cases in which parents had to leave and live alone to avoid this.

Returning to thoughts expressed in *Down and Out in London and Paris*, Orwell wrote that lengthy unemployment robs a person of hope. Even though they have plenty of time, they no longer have the incentive to fill it productively. This had even happened to talented writers he had known who had hit hard times. Why don't they "sit down and write books? . . . Because to write books you need not only comfort and solitude . . . you also need peace of mind."[18]

Orwell had become aware of England's "unemployment problem" when he returned from Burma. The economy was strong immediately after World War I, when he had left England. By 1928, times were bad, especially in the northern industrial parts of the country. What "horrified and amazed" Orwell was that many men were ashamed of being out of work. They had been brought up to work and were "haunted by a feeling of personal degradation."[19]

Eventually, he observed, they realized it was not their fault. Without much prospect of jobs, unemployment became a way of life. To their detriment, in his view, many went without necessities rather than luxuries. Thus, people bought radios and paid for electricity but went without sufficient food. Cheap luxuries, such as the

A man rides his bicycle along Wigan Pier in January 2000. By the turn of the twenty-first century, Wigan had become a prosperous town.

movies and Britain's long-running national lottery, the Football Pools, had helped to distract the working class from its troubles. Orwell remarked that "we are sometimes told that the whole thing is an astute manoeuvre by the governing class . . . to hold the unemployed down."[20]

Food, like entertainment, was used by the unemployed as a distraction from their circumstances, he wrote. They wanted something tasty to eat, and were not interested in whether it had nutritional value. The typical diet was "appalling," said Orwell, and consisted of "white bread and margarine, corned beef, sugared tea and potatoes."[21]

77

"The results of all this," Orwell continued, "are visible in a physical degeneracy." The decline he blamed partly on World War I, which "had taken the million best men in England and slaughtered them, largely before they had had time to breed." Overall, he concluded, "the English working class do not show much capacity for leadership, but they have a wonderful talent for organization. The whole trade union movement testifies to this."[22]

Orwell was conscious that as a middle-class southerner he could not expect to be accepted easily by northern workers. His accent, for one thing, would set him apart. Jerry Kennan, his host in Wigan, remembered him as "very cynical" and "a snob . . . [who] was trying to come down to earth and find out what things [were] really like."[23]

In one way, though, he would surely have fit right in. He commented on the straightforwardness of working people, and that's a quality that resonates through his writing. Except when he was describing the industrial landscape, he rarely wandered far from plain language.

One memorable passage is his vision of the steel-making city of Sheffield at night with "serrated flames, like circular saws," squeezing out of foundry chimneys. Through the foundries' open doors he saw "fiery serpents of iron being hauled to and fro" and "the scream of the iron" under the blows of steam hammers.[24]

Orwell returned to the subject of class differences frequently. He likened it to "the plate-glass pane of an aquarium; it is so easy to pretend that it isn't there, and so impossible to get through it."[25]

Even writers deluded themselves and others into thinking they were not affected by class differences, he noted. "Every novelist of serious pretensions adopts an ironic attitude towards his upper-class characters," Orwell wrote. The speech of "educated" people had become so lifeless, he added, that novelists can only ridicule it.[26]

A New Home and a New Wife

Orwell and Eileen were married on June 9, 1936. Eileen, three years younger than Orwell, gave up studying for her master's degree and spent the rest of her life for the most part playing a supporting role in her husband's career.

While Orwell was writing *The Road to Wigan Pier*, the decidedly mixed reviews started to come out for *Keep the Aspidistra Flying*. Orwell's old school friend Cyril Connolly compared it unfavorably to *Burmese Days*, claiming that Orwell's distaste for London tainted the new novel.[27] American publisher Harper & Brothers did not publish it until 1956, concluding at the time Orwell finished the novel that it was "too British" to sell well in the United States.[28]

By the time *The Road to Wigan Pier* was published in March 1937, however, Orwell had already embarked on another journey. When civil war broke out in Spain between fascists and socialists, Orwell felt he had to stand up for his beliefs. In mid-December he left England for Spain, ready to fight, or write, in defense of socialism.

WAR IN EUROPE

Examining *Homage to Catalonia* and *Coming Up for Air*

As a writer whose focus was politics and social inequality, George Orwell was inevitably drawn to the Spanish Civil War, which lasted from 1936 until 1939. For him, as for many of his generation, it was the watershed event in the ideological struggle between socialism and fascism.

As Orwell wrote in *Homage To Catalonia*, "here at last, apparently, was democracy standing up to fascism. For years past the so-called democratic countries had been surrendering to fascism at every step."[1]

The various socialist and communist factions which fought against fascism did not always share the same beliefs or get along with each other. But initially one thing they did have in common, in addition to their hatred of fascists, was that they looked to the Soviet Union for leadership.

Revolutionaries from around the world were inspired by the Soviet example, and many fought to defend the Spanish Republican government when it was threatened in 1936 by an uprising led by General Francisco Franco. Government supporters were called Loyalists. The so-called Nationalist opposition included fascists.

The Nationalist cause represented the old social order. It drew support from the landed aristocracy, owners of big businesses, and the Roman Catholic church. The fascist governments of Italy and Germany contributed troops and weapons to Franco's armies.

The war began in July 1936 when General Franco started a revolt in Spain's North African colony of Morocco. From there he invaded Spain to help right-wing rebels fight against the government.

Orwell arrived in Spain's northeastern province of Catalonia in December 1936. Initially, he said later, he intended to write about the war for British newspapers. Whatever his intentions were in going to Spain, he soon became so committed to the socialist cause that he joined in the fighting.[2]

At first, the Loyalist or Republican army consisted mainly of militias, each affiliated with a trade union or political party. Orwell joined P.O.U.M., a militia that supported anarchist politics and was connected with the Workers' Party of Marxist Unity ("Partido Obrero de Unificación Marxista"). He chose this militia because it had connections with people he knew in a small English socialist party, the Independent Labour Party (ILP). The

ILP had once been part of the socialist movement from which the current British Labour Party grew.

Both socialists and anarchists were strongly represented in Catalonia and its principal city, Barcelona. Rivalry between the two political factions eventually turned into open conflict and was a major theme in Orwell's book.

The revolutionary atmosphere in Barcelona when Orwell arrived left a vivid impression on him. The red and black flags of the anarchists waved everywhere, and workers were in control. Buildings and private cars had been taken over, and apparently "the wealthy classes had practically ceased to exist. . . . There was much in it that I did not understand," Orwell wrote, and "in some ways I did not even like it, but I recognized it immediately as a state of affairs worth fighting for."[3]

This idyllic situation, as it must have been regarded from an anarchist standpoint, did not last. The growing contrast between conditions in Barcelona and those at the front where the fighting was going on began to have an effect on the war effort.

When he first joined P.O.U.M., Orwell had assumed that differences between the Loyalist groups were minor in the face of the common fascist threat. But that proved not to be the case. The socialists and communists eventually suppressed the anarchists, imprisoning and shooting some of their leaders.

JOINING UP IN BARCELONA

When Orwell first entered Barcelona, however, there was still a sense that everyone was equal. Even women had gained a measure of equality, and were trained to fight in the army alongside the men.

Not everything about the city met with Orwell's approval though. It had "the evil atmosphere of war," he wrote, with food shortages, dim street lighting because of the danger of air raids, and buildings in disrepair.[4] But Orwell was impressed by the friendliness and candor of the people, even though he had to struggle to make himself understood. He did not speak much Spanish at first. In addition, many of his comrades spoke to each other in Catalan, the language of Catalonia.

Orwell estimated that half of his unit was under the age of sixteen. Military training was inadequate, to say the least, and there was such a shortage of rifles that troops arriving at the front line had to take the rifles of the soldiers they were relieving. There were many delays before the recruits were transported to the front.

"Whenever it is conceivably possible, the business of today is put off until mañana," Orwell commented.[5] Eventually, his company went by truck, or "lorry" to use the British term, to a part of the line at the village of Alcubierre, near the city of Zaragoza, in the region of Aragon and not far from the Spanish border with France.

A few Nationalist deserters gave Orwell his first contact with the enemy. Apart from different uniforms, he noted, "they were indistinguishable from ourselves." This part of the fascist line was held by "wretched conscripts . . . [who] were only too anxious to escape."[6]

On the third morning rifles were issued to Orwell's unit, and he was dismayed to find that his, like all the others, was forty years old and in poor condition. Not surprisingly, the unit's first casualty was self-inflicted, when the cartridge case in one of the rifles exploded.

At first, there was very little fighting, and the main adversaries were the cold, discomfort, and boredom. Orwell listed the priorities in warfare as being firewood, food, tobacco, candles, and the enemy—in that order.

In one respect at least, the anarchists in Catalonia seemed to have had an advantage over the fascists. Their food was distinctly better, so much so that Loyalist propagandists tried to persuade the enemy to desert by shouting across the lines that they had buttered toast as part of their rations.

Typically, there are few frills in Orwell's memoir of Spain. Once again, metaphors and similes stand out all the more for being so rare. There is a rather poetic description of Orwell's natural surroundings, soon after his arrival at the front, in which he referred to "the green beaks of wild crocuses or irises poking through" the soil on the hillsides and the first streaks of dawn "like swords slitting the darkness."[7]

From Alcubierre, Orwell and his fellow anarchist militiamen were transferred to a part of the line facing the town of Huesca. Evidently the front was quiet. When Orwell came to write his account several months later he

General Francisco Franco became dictator of Spain in 1939 after leading the rebel Nationalist Army to victory over Loyalist forces in the Spanish Civil War.

used this segment to sketch the background to the war as he saw it. Partly his intention was to counteract coverage by the British newspapers, which he felt were not reporting the war accurately.

The anarchists and socialists who dominated the trade unions in Spain had been the first effective opponents of Franco's military revolt, he wrote. But their revolutionary ideas were ignored or opposed by virtually everyone else, including the communists, their fellow Loyalists.

As Orwell explained it, the Soviet Union controlled communist opinion everywhere. Their top priority was self-preservation in the face of Nazi Germany's growing power. Britain and France, though capitalist and anticommunist, were potential allies against Germany. Therefore, those countries' financial interests in Spain had to be protected from the anarchists, who tended to seize private property and generally opposed capitalism.

The official Communist Party policy then was that revolution would be premature in Spain. Until fascism was defeated, the Communist goal would be to support parliamentary democracy in Spain.

In late 1936, control of the Spanish Government began to swing toward the communists and away from the anarchists.

"Philosophically," Orwell wrote, "Communism and Anarchism are poles apart. . . . The Communist's emphasis is always on centralism and efficiency, the Anarchist's on liberty and equality."[8]

In time, this power struggle reflected political divisions

that had occurred earlier in the Soviet Union. Dictator Joseph Stalin had driven his former revolutionary comrade, Leon Trotsky, into exile. Spanish anarchists came to be branded as "Trotskyists" by the communists, and ultimately many were accused of being traitors and imprisoned.

Orwell returned to his account of life at the front with more description of day-to-day conditions. To add to other discomforts, lice were a constant presence in the clothing and on the bodies of the soldiers.

A few days in hospital as the result of a minor infection gave Orwell a break from the monotonous conditions. There was even an actual attack on an enemy position. All the same, when he went on leave after 115 days on the front line, Orwell felt much of his time in Spain had been wasted. Later, he changed his mind and savored this period as one in which people had briefly been able to live according to socialist principles.

TROTSKYISM— *Named after the Russian revolutionary Leon Trotsky, who believed the working classes should lead a worldwide communist revolution.*

"Many of the normal motives of civilized life—snobbishness, money-grubbing, fear of the boss, etc.—had simply ceased to exist," he recalled. "Of course such a state of affairs could not last. . . . But it lasted long enough to have its effect upon anyone who experienced it . . . the Spanish militias, while they lasted, were a sort of microcosm of a classless society."[9]

A BRIEF UTOPIA

As with so many utopias, this one did not last long. Orwell returned to Barcelona when his unit was relieved at the front, and found that the revolutionary spirit was virtually gone. Class differences were evident once again. The blue overalls and militia uniforms of the workers and anarchists had given way to smart suits and summer dresses. Also, the residents of the city, which was relatively far from the fighting, seemed to be losing interest in the war. In his dirty, battered uniform, Orwell felt out of place.

Political and military changes added to Orwell's concern that the anarchists were losing influence. The Government was organizing a new Popular Army to replace the militias. The anarchists of the P.O.U.M. militia had been fighting as the Lenin Division, named after Stalin's predecessor as leader of the Soviet Union. The division was to be known in the future by ideologically neutral numerals—as the 29th.

Worst of all was the tension between communists and anarchists. In May 1937, the police and anarchists in Barcelona began shooting at each other. To complicate things further, there were three types of police roaming the city—the Guardia Civil or national police; the Asaltos or the riot or assault police; and the Carabineros or the frontier guards.

The immediate cause of friction, in Orwell's opinion, was a Republican Government order to surrender all private weapons. In addition, trade union members were excluded from being in the police. Many feared that the

Government would take away the unions' control of important industries next. There was, said Orwell, "a general vague feeling that the revolution had been sabotaged."[10]

Orwell returned to the front line with much less optimism about the outcome of the war. He still believed the Republican Government was better than a fascist victory. The Government would at least be "anti feudal" and "keep the Church in check," he wrote.[11] It would promote education and public health, and the peasants were more likely to keep land that had been taken from the wealthy and given to them.

There were disturbing signs of things to come, however. A leading British supporter of P.O.U.M., Bob Smillie, had been arrested by the Government. He was imprisoned in the city of Valencia, where the Government was then headquartered after the Nationalists laid siege to the Spanish capital, Madrid. There was also less equality in the militias. Orwell was made a *teniente*, about the same in rank as a second lieutenant.

He did not have long to get used to his promotion. Early one day in mid-June Orwell was shot through the throat. There was a loud bang and a blinding flash, he wrote: "no pain, only a violent shock."[12]

An American volunteer came to his aid, and he was carried by stretcher to a doctor. By that time he was starting to feel pain, but he tried not to complain because blood bubbled out of his mouth when he did. Conditions in the hospitals immediately behind the lines were predictably bad, the notable perk being good food.

Orwell endured multiple examinations by doctors. He was told he was lucky to be alive, and that he would never get his voice back. But after a couple of months of whispering, he was able to speak properly again—although never with the same strength as before.

Returning to Barcelona, Orwell found that P.O.U.M. members were increasingly persecuted by the Government guard units. Major Georges Kopp, a Belgian who was commander of Orwell's militia unit, was among those imprisoned. Orwell tried unsuccessfully to get him out, at some risk to himself. After trying for a while, he suspected—wrongly as it turned out—Kopp had been shot by the police. The friendship between the two men survived the war at any rate, and Kopp later moved to England.

As a result of his wound, Orwell was eligible for a medical discharge from the militia. He went to P.O.U.M. militia headquarters near the front to make it official, and then returned to Barcelona. His wife was waiting for him at their hotel. Her first words to him when they met in the lobby were a whisper to get out. As she pushed him out of the hotel, she explained that the police were arresting anyone known to be a P.O.U.M. member. Orwell was no longer safe in his old haunts. Their hotel room had already been searched, and his diaries and letters confiscated.

Orwell felt relatively safe during the day. But at night, when the police raids took place, he had to hide on the streets and sleep outside. Virtually anything was better than being put in the Spanish jails, by Orwell's account. They were like dungeons, he explained. Some prisoners went months without seeing daylight, and daily rations for many consisted of two bowls of soup and two pieces of bread.

Still, Orwell kept his high opinion of Spaniards in general. He had many bad memories of Spain, he wrote, but very few bad memories of its people. Only twice did he get "seriously angry" with a Spaniard, he recalled, and looking back he believed he was wrong both times.[13]

GOING HOME

Finally, Orwell, his wife, and a couple of friends were able to slip over the French border by train. All he carried with him from his six months in Spain was a goatskin water bottle and a tiny oil lamp he had picked out of a ruined hut during the fighting. His first action in France was to buy cigars and cigarettes from a tobacco kiosk. It took a few days to get used to being able to buy tobacco whenever he wanted to.

After a few days of rest and reflection in a French fishing village, Orwell and his wife set out for England. However it turned out, he was sure the war would be a disaster for Spain. And yet, "curiously enough the whole experience has left me with not less but more belief in the decency of human beings."[14]

Passing through Paris, he noted the changes there. On

his way to Spain, he had felt the city had become "decayed and gloomy" since he was there gathering material for *Down and Out in Paris and London* eight years before. A poor economy had closed many cafes and people were worried about the prospect of war with Germany. Now, on his return a few months later, Paris seemed "gay and prosperous" compared to Spain.[15]

The peaceful countryside of southern England, on the other hand, looked untouched by Europe's problems. Even the industrial conditions of the north that Orwell had described in *The Road To Wigan Pier* were many miles away. "It was still the England I had known in my childhood," Orwell concluded, ". . . sleeping the deep, deep sleep of England, from which I sometimes fear that we shall never wake till we are jerked out of it by the roar of bombs."[16]

By the end of June Orwell was back in London, and lost little time combating what he considered to be distortions and lies about what was happening in Spain. But the ideological splits in the Republican ranks that Orwell had witnessed in Barcelona were just as evident on the pages of British newspapers. Orwell had trouble getting his views accepted, or published.[17] Even his former publisher Victor Gollancz shied away,[18] and Orwell had to turn to another firm, Secker & Warburg, to put out *Homage to Catalonia*.

The book was finished in January 1938, when Orwell and Eileen were once again living in their rural refuge in

Wallington. It was published in April 1938 in England, although not until 1952 in the United States.

To Orwell's surprise, however, the book failed to sell well despite some favorable reviews.[19] Biographer Michael Shelden speculates that the public was overwhelmed by books about the war, and that Orwell's detailed background about politics and the militias overloaded his narrative.[20] Without these explanations from Orwell though, the account of the complicated war would be difficult to understand, particularly so many years later.

The book's reception did not stop Orwell revisiting the subject in an essay published in 1943, "Looking Back on the Spanish War." The essay examined how propaganda and bias had distorted the way events had been portrayed. Orwell mused that the fascists who had won in Spain would determine how the history of that war was written. In a sentence that foreshadowed themes in *Animal Farm* and *1984*, he wrote that "for all practical purposes the lie will have become truth."[21]

In another hint of what was to come in *1984*, Orwell put his faith in the working class as the true hope of resistance against totalitarianism. He likened the working class to a plant which "is blind and stupid, but it knows enough to keep pushing upwards towards the light."[22]

The essay concludes with a poem Orwell had written in memory of an Italian militiaman mentioned at the beginning of *Homage to Catalonia*. The Italian was one of the first soldiers Orwell met when he enlisted in P.O.U.M., and obviously made a deep impression.

But the thing that I saw in your face
No power can disinherit;
No bomb that ever burst
Shatters the crystal spirit.[23]

ANOTHER NOVEL

After the documentary treatment of his experiences in Spain, Orwell returned to the form of the novel for his next book, *Coming Up for Air*. First, though, he had to decide what to do about an offer he had received from a newspaper publisher in the city of Lucknow, India. The publisher offered Orwell a position as an assistant editor, a job that included writing opinion pieces. With India's growing independence movement creating political excitement, the opportunity was tempting. Orwell considered the prospect of a book about India coming out of the experience.

As it turned out, the decision was taken out of Orwell's hands by ill health. A cough turned into something worse. Once again, Orwell's lungs were causing him problems. Eileen recruited her brother Laurence, a surgeon, to admit Orwell into a sanatorium, a convalescent home.[24] His illness was enough to make him remark in a letter to his friend Cyril Connolly that he had not expected to write another novel.[25] Not until the summer of 1938 was he ready to think much about writing again.

His progress on *Coming Up for Air* was accompanied by a dramatic change of scene. Believing a warmer, drier climate might help his recovery, Eileen and Orwell spent several months in Morocco—then a French colony—renting a house near the city of Marrakech.

Judging by letters he wrote to friends in England, he did not enjoy his new surroundings. In one, he described Morocco as "rather a dull country," and in another commented that the social hierarchy reminded him of Anglo-Indian society.[26] An essay from this period, entitled "Marrakech," focused on these perceived inequalities between rulers and ruled. His homesickness was augmented by gloomy prophesies about the approaching war with Hitler.

By the time the couple returned to England in June 1939, Orwell was ready to deliver the manuscript of his new book to Victor Gollancz. Once again, personal setbacks mixed with professional life. Orwell's father died of cancer later that month. It was some consolation to Orwell that his father had taken more interest in his son's writing toward the end of his life.[27]

On the political stage, Europe was moving ever closer to war. When Stalin and Hitler reached an agreement in August not to attack each other—leaving Germany free to invade neighboring countries—many leftists felt betrayed by Stalin. (World War II would begin with the German invasion of Poland on September 1, 1939.)

For Orwell as for others, it was no longer possible to oppose war. Britain had to be defended against totalitarianism, whether it be the Nazi or the communist version.[28]

COMING UP FOR AIR

Orwell included his nightmare vision of the anticipated war in *Coming Up for Air*. As with his previous novels, the book draws significantly from his own background. Not that his protagonist, George 'Fatty' Bowling, has Orwell's experiences exactly. For one thing, Orwell set Bowling's birth date in 1893, ten years before his own. But Orwell did draw from character types, places, and situations not so far from his own memories.

Above all, *Coming Up for Air* gave Orwell a chance to reminisce about the big changes in England following World War I. The narrative is shaped by Bowling's recollections of his life.

Orwell set his story in the same period in which he was writing—the late 1930s. George Bowling is a forty-five-year-old insurance salesman. He lives in a southern English suburb called West Bletchley, with his wife Hilda and two children, seven-year-old Billy and eleven-year-old Lorna. Their home on Ellesmere Road is much like the others in a long row of little semidetached houses. Home, family, and job—George is a bit jaded about all of that. At times he feels like "a tame dairy-cow" at the beck and call of his family. But his children can also inspire devotion.[29]

A new set of false teeth has started George thinking about his appearance. Although he acknowledges putting on a little too much weight in recent years, he feels he is not "such a bad figure of a man." With his "bricky" red face, butter-colored hair and pale-blue eyes, he can still convince himself sometimes that women might find him attractive.[30]

George's imagination ricochets between his past and prophetic visions of England's future. As in his previous two books, Orwell predicted the war that was to become all too real very shortly. George, like Gordon Comstock in *Keep the Aspidistra Flying*, imagines air raids over England. Confrontation with fascism seems inevitable. London is a sitting duck for the bombs.

All is not gloomy for George though. A bet he made on a racehorse has paid off well. His wager of "ten bob"—10 shillings—has won him 17 quid, slang for 17 pounds. It was a good amount in British money in the 1930s, and enables George to plan a visit to Lower Binfield, the town where he was born and where he lived until he was a young man.

His father had owned a small shop in Lower Binfield, and sold seeds and supplies for local farmers and horse owners. But George's parents were creatures of routine, and were unprepared for change. A combination of cars and competition put a strain on the family business. Just before he was sixteen, George had to leave school to contribute to the family income. He worked at a grocer's shop for six years. His elder brother Joe, meanwhile, left home and was never in contact with the family again.

George's memories of childhood and youth are mostly good. He loved fishing and reading, and for a while he lived with a girl named Elsie Waters. The coming of war in July 1914 changed everything. He enlisted in the British

Army and was wounded by shrapnel. While he was serving in France his father died, followed not long after by his mother. As he thinks back twenty years to when he was last in Lower Binfield—for his mother's funeral—George decides he will spend his windfall on a trip to his birthplace.

Telling Hilda that he needs to be away for a few days because of his job, he drives instead to Lower Binfield. Because of all the growth, he hardly recognizes the place. What was a small country market town by the River Thames has acquired a couple of factories and a population of newcomers. About the only place that has not changed is the church, although now gravestones have replaced the faces once so familiar to him. After a few days absorbing all this, George heads for home, steeling himself to face Hilda and perhaps having to admit the truth about where he has been.

Coming Up for Air may be most effective if approached as a social document. It does not have an action-packed plot. George's state of mind, like his nation's, is stuck in the past, despite the change in the places he knows. Character development is limited to his rather depressing conclusion that there is no point in worrying about life's bigger issues. Not very many people do. "What's the future got to do with chaps like you and me?" he asks himself. "Holding down our jobs—that's our future. As for Hilda, even when the bombs are dropping she'll still be thinking about the price of butter."[31]

As an account of someone living in England in the mid-1930s, it makes interesting reading. World War I had already brought about big social and political shifts in Europe. The Depression of the 1930s and the prospect of another world war were shaking things up again.

Sales of the new novel were markedly better than they had been for Orwell's book about Spain. Buoyed by encouraging reviews, *Coming Up for Air* quickly sold out its 2,000 printing and more copies had to be printed. Of the reviews, one of the more intriguing opinions came much later, from biographer Bernard Crick. He speculated that Orwell may have written about a lower middle-class protagonist in order to appeal to just that class of reader, hoping to inspire them "to assert themselves and the real England."[32]

WAR WORK

When Britain declared war on Germany on September 3, 1939, Orwell focused on supporting the war effort. He had been considering a trilogy of novels, "a family saga sort of thing," with a tentative title of *The Quick and the Dead*.[33] Instead, he turned back to the shorter material that was his staple—essays and book reviews for various magazines. To these he added regular columns for an American magazine to which he had been invited to contribute, the *Partisan Review*.

In March 1940, three of his essays were published in a collection entitled *Inside the Whale*. In addition to the title piece, it contained a long analysis of the novels of Charles Dickens and "Boys' Weeklies," Orwell's observations on the world of comic papers. In the latter, he reflected on how these papers portrayed popular taste and standards. Dickens, with his concern for social conditions, had an obvious appeal for Orwell. The collection further enhanced Orwell's reputation as an essayist, with one reviewer referring to him as "a man of letters."[34]

More recognition came with another essay, "The Lion and the Unicorn." Taking its title from the British Royal Coat of Arms, this long essay gauges the state of the nation as Orwell saw it after the first full year of war. It begins with an assessment of the English character, progresses to criticism of the leadership that had allowed the country to drift into war largely unprepared, and culminates by stating that Western democracy, no matter how flawed, is greatly preferable to fascism.

In the course of his argument, Orwell attacked a couple of his perennial targets—the "idle rich" and leftist intellectuals, whom he accused of being apologists for totalitarian states. He was convinced that victory in the war and the establishment of socialism in Britain were inseparable, and he put forward a six-part plan to help bring this about. Among his recommendations were nationalization of the means of economic production and reform of the colonial system.

The essay spelled out his commitment to a uniquely English form of democratic socialism, a system subject to law. It also underlined Orwell's attachment to his country and willingness to fight for it if the cause were just. His poor health had prevented him joining Britain's main military forces, but he did become a member of the Home Guard, a grassroots defense force formed to resist any Nazi invasion.

Orwell's predictions in this essay about the inevitability of socialism and its replacement of capitalism have proven to be inaccurate. But as insight into his state of mind, the essay is invaluable. Critics applauded its optimism, and praised Orwell as "a socialist and a patriot—a rare combination."[35] There was even an invitation to speak at Oxford University.[36]

Although Orwell was eager to reveal his political thinking, he was less forthcoming about his personal life during this period and wrote little about it. At the start of the war, Eileen had taken a job as a government censor, living at her brother Laurence's house in London. Orwell remained at the cottage in Wallington before the couple eventually rented a place in the city.

Two personal losses evidently affected Eileen deeply. In May 1940, her brother Laurence was killed during the British Army's catastrophic evacuation of Dunkirk in France. Ironically, her brother—an army surgeon with a particular interest in chest injuries—died of just such a wound.[37] The following year her mother died.

For two years, from August 1941 until September 1943, Orwell worked as a radio producer for the British Broadcasting Corporation's Empire Department. His job was to counter German propaganda aimed primarily at India. He had to write reports about war developments and read them over the radio. Later, second wife, Sonia, called his time at the BBC "perhaps the bleakest period of his life." Only after he left to become literary editor of the Socialist newspaper *Tribune* did he have much time to devote to his own books again.[38]

Friends and colleagues from this time apparently had mixed impressions of Orwell. He could be quick to criticize, and on several occasions withdrew hasty accusations about the political loyalties or competence of other writers. However, he was not prepared to apologize after writing that science fiction pioneer H.G.Wells was out of touch. Wells had been a boyhood hero for Orwell, but that did not prevent a heated confrontation at a dinner party after Orwell's remarks had been printed.[39] He too reached a point at which he concluded he could be more effective writing in another capacity and he resigned from the BBC in 1943.[40]

The year 1943 was an eventful one for Orwell. His mother died in March. Then, in November, he began writing *Animal Farm*, his satire of Stalinist Russia. He already had a busy schedule writing reviews and columns for various publications. But this was not to be a long book, and he completed it in three months.[41]

His workload did not interfere with a happy event in his personal life. In June 1944, the Orwells adopted a son, Richard Horatio. Orwell's wish for a child had been growing for some time, and the couple had not been able to have one of their own.[42]

It took more than a year to find a publisher for *Animal Farm*, the result of dramatic shifts in the progress of the war. When Hitler broke his nonaggression pact and invaded the Soviet Union in 1941, Stalin was suddenly transformed from turncoat to ally in the minds of many influential people in British government and literary circles.

Several publishers, including Victor Gollancz and once again T.S. Eliot at Faber & Faber, turned down *Animal Farm* because it seemed to them to be critical of Britain's ally.[43] When eventually it was published, by Secker & Warburg in August 1945, *Animal Farm* completely vindicated Orwell's faith in it. Favorable reviews and strong sales were mirrored in the United States when the book was published there the following year. World events once again had played a part. With the war over, the victorious allies were divided by the cold war. Stalin was again a figure to be feared and distrusted.

COLD WAR—*A confrontation that stops short of military conflict, such as the classic standoff between the United States with its allies and the Soviet Union and its Communist satellites in the second half of the twentieth century.*

A POLITICAL FABLE

Examining *Animal Farm*

Although *Animal Farm* satirizes the Russian Revolution, Orwell clearly had larger targets in mind too. The theme of a revolution being betrayed by its leaders and the role of power in politics have universal relevance, and Orwell said and wrote as much.[1]

The motivation for writing the book apparently went back as far as the streets of Barcelona, when Orwell witnessed revolutionary propaganda and infighting first-hand. He wanted to write about this in a way that would be easily understood by a wide readership. In *Animal Farm*, he would succeed in this more than he could have imagined.

The idea of using animals in an allegory or fable occurred to him, he explained, after watching a boy driving a cart horse along a country path with a whip. "It struck me that if only such animals became aware of their strength we should have no power over them."[2]

THE POLITICAL CONTEXT

Orwell was writing against a background of ideological struggle in Europe going back to the turn of the last century. The communist revolution in Russia and the triumph of fascism in Germany, Italy, and Spain had culminated in a devastating war.

Writers were as split by the conflict as the rest of the population, as Orwell indicated in his essay "Inside the Whale," with its criticism of Henry Miller's lack of political involvement. Orwell, of course, had participated in the battle between the two ideologies. But he had become disillusioned with communism under the Soviet leader Joseph Stalin.

Under Stalin, communism had been tarnished by hypocrisy and tyranny. Stalin's treatment of people who disagreed with him could be just as ruthless and cruel as the methods of the Russian monarchs, the czars, before the revolution.

When Orwell finished his book early in 1944, many people in Western Europe and the United States did not want to hear about this dark side. Not only was Stalin their ally but for many of those on the political left he was a hero and role model.

With Germany defeated in 1945, however, Soviet relations with its former allies of World War II, the United States and Britain, changed drastically. The Soviets were no longer portrayed as heroes. Instead they were regarded as the oppressors of countries they had invaded and occupied in Eastern Europe.

The hostility was to reach a critical point in mid 1948 when Soviet troops blocked roads to Berlin. The former German capital city, surrounded by Soviet-controlled East Germany, was divided into a western part, administered by the Allies, and an eastern part under Soviet command.

For many months, the United States and Britain could only airlift supplies of food, fuel, and other necessities to West Berlin residents and their own garrisons. Years later, the Soviet Union built a wall to isolate their part of Berlin from the rest of the West.

With a phrase made famous by British politician Winston Churchill, Europe was divided by an "iron curtain." This state of hostility was called the cold war—a term, incidentally, reported to have been first used by Orwell.[3] The wall was smashed down by Germans themselves late in 1989 and the Soviet Union fell apart in 1991. The Soviet system, it turned out, was not so powerful and long lasting as Orwell's story suggested it might be.

The relevance of *Animal Farm* is not limited to any single revolution though. That is one of the reasons it continues to be read and valued so highly. It is a story about power and privilege and human nature. It is about individuals and how they react differently and find different roles within a community. As such, it is as relevant to today's revolutions and tyrannies as it was to those in Orwell's day.

The critical and public acclaim that followed British publication in August 1945—and the following year in the United States— reflected a wide range of opinion. There were those who read the book as a condemnation of all forms of socialism and those who regarded the Soviet Union as its only target. Almost without exception, though, critics recognized the book's importance.

Such was the enthusiasm that Orwell felt it necessary to clarify what he had intended to convey. Some readers, for example, interpreted the ending as a show of harmony between pigs and humans. Orwell expected relations between the Soviet Union and the West to sour after the end of the war, and wanted his story to leave readers sensing this mutual suspicion.[4]

ORWELL'S USE OF ALLEGORY

Animal Farm is both an allegory and a fable. The story fits the definition of an allegory because it uses fictional characters and events to represent or symbolize people and events in the real world. The use of animals as characters in a story to make a point gives *Animal Farm* the qualities of a fable.

The story is about a group of animals who take over the farm on which they live. The farm is clearly intended to be understood as Russia, with the humans and animals in the story representing various people caught up in the revolution. Some of the animals have a close parallel with specific people; others are more akin to general types or classes within the population.

For example, the pigs Napoleon and Snowball bring to

mind the Soviet leaders Joseph Stalin and Leon Trotsky, respectively. There are aspects of the pigs' personalities as well as things that happen to them that have close counterparts in the real events of the Russian Revolution.

On the other hand, the cart horse Boxer is more representative of the working class in general than a specific individual. The sheep and dogs are other animals in the story that function as types and aspects of society rather than individual characters.

Orwell was certainly not the first writer to use an allegory to criticize political and social events. One of his favorite writers, Jonathan Swift, had used the same approach to express his views of eighteenth-century politics in his book *Gulliver's Travels*. For that matter, Orwell would have been familiar with a long tradition of using animal fables to highlight aspects of human life.[5] It is an effective form because it allows the writer to concentrate on the essence of the story without getting bogged down in factual detail.

If Orwell had written a history of the Russian Revolution, he no doubt would have made the same points about the leaders betraying the ideals for which they had initially fought. That would have required a great deal of research about dates, names, and sequences of events. With an allegory, he could focus on the message. The relative simplicity of the story makes it memorable and gives it impact.

Orwell was as economical with language as he was focused with his plot. He used no more descriptive words and passages than he needed to keep his narrative moving. The form of the allegory suits his style.

LIFE ON THE FARM

At the beginning of Orwell's story, Animal Farm is known as Manor Farm and is owned by Mr. Jones. One night, after Mr. and Mrs. Jones have gone to bed, the animals meet in the barn. Major, a boar nearing the end of his life, has had a dream he wants to share.

Among those assembled are the horses Boxer and the motherly mare Clover; the three dogs Bluebell, Jessie, and Pincher; the goat Muriel; the donkey Benjamin; the foolish, pretty mare Mollie; the cat; the tame raven Moses; and an assortment of pigs, sheep, cows, hens, and ducklings.

Major announces that before he dies he wants to share his reflections about life. The plain truth, he says, is that "the life of an animal is misery and slavery." Farm animals are fed only enough to keep them alive, and are expected to work until their strength gives out. Finally, when they are no longer useful, they are "slaughtered with hideous cruelty."[6]

This does not have to be the case, Major continues. England's soil and climate could produce more than enough food. The animals' deprived condition is because "nearly the whole of the produce of our labor is stolen from us by human beings."[7]

"Man is the only real enemy we have," Major says.

Without Man, hunger and overwork would not exist. "Man is the only creature that consumes without producing."[8]

Sooner or later, Major declares, Man must be overthrown.

There is a brief interruption in the speech when four rats emerge and the dogs give chase. Prompted by Major, the farm animals then vote that in the future wild animals will be treated as their friends.

Major winds up his address by listing a set of guidelines. Whatever goes upon two legs is an enemy; whatever goes upon four legs, or has wings, is a friend. Even when animals have driven away humans, he tells them, they must never adopt Man's evil ways, such as living in houses, sleeping in beds, wearing clothes, drinking alcohol, smoking, or dealing with money or trade. Above all, no animal should ever oppress or kill other animals. All animals are equal.

Finally, Major talks about a dream he had "of the earth as it will be when Man has vanished." An old song, called "Beasts of England," had come back to him in the dream too. It describes a "golden future" in which animals are free of Man's control.[9] Following Major's lead, all the animals sing. The noise wakes Mr. Jones, however, and the animals quickly flee to their sleeping places.

Major is a prophet of revolution. In this, he's a combination of Karl Marx, nineteenth-century author of the *Communist Manifesto* and *Das Kapital*, and Vladimir Lenin, the political leader who led the Russian Revolution. Like

Marx, Major puts forward the theories which lead to action.

Major does not live to see his visions take effect. Three nights after the meeting, he dies in his sleep. It is left to the two younger boars, Napoleon and Snowball, to take up the cause. Their chief helper is another young pig named Squealer, whose role is to explain decisions and policy to the other animals.

With Major's speech as a basis, these new ideas are given the name Animalism. The pigs take the lead in educating the other animals. They sometimes have to argue against the old ways of life on the farm, such as working loyally for the humans. It is hard to convince the mare Mollie, for instance, that the sugar and ribbons she likes so much are symbols of her dependence on Mr. Jones.

The raven Moses is a particular problem for the pigs. He is Mr. Jones' pet and is considered to be a spy and a clever talker. He claims to know of a country up in the sky called Sugarcandy Mountain, where animals go after they die. There they could rest and eat their favorite foods. The pigs, Orwell wrote, "had to argue very hard to persuade them that there was no such place."[10]

Some animals take readily to Animalism. The two cart horses Boxer and Clover are the most devoted. They are emotionally drawn to its ideas even though they do not have much grasp of the finer points. Others, notably the sheep, bleat slogans and follow directions mindlessly.

The revolution comes sooner and is accomplished easier than expected. Upset by losing money in a lawsuit,

Mr. Jones has started drinking. He neglects his farm, and his employees start to shirk. On Midsummer's Eve, Mr. Jones gets drunk and forgets to feed the animals, who then break into the feed and start to help themselves. Mr. Jones and his four men arrive with whips and lash out at the animals. But, driven by hunger, the animals retaliate.

Spontaneously they butt and kick Mr. Jones and his men, who flee. Seeing what is happening from the farmhouse, Mrs. Jones grabs a few possessions and follows her husband into exile. Here the plot conforms to the gist of what happened during the Russian Revolution rather than following events to the letter. Mr. and Mrs. Jones leave the farm alive. In the real-life Russian Revolution, the Russian ruling family was executed. It takes a while for the animals to come to terms with their new freedom. After galloping around the farm to make sure there are no humans left on it, they destroy the tools and equipment that were used to control them. Harnesses, dog chains, whips, and even ribbons are thrown away. The next day they look around the farmhouse. Mollie adorns herself with some ribbon she found, much to the others' disapproval.

The pigs reveal that they have learned to read and write from a book they found in the farmhouse. Snowball, who is best at writing, paints a new name on the entrance gate to the farm. In place of Manor Farm, he writes Animal Farm.

They have also drawn up Seven Commandments to represent the central principles of Animalism. These are based on Major's directions that whatever goes upon two legs is an enemy; whatever goes upon four legs, or has wings, is a friend; no animal shall wear clothes, sleep in a bed, drink alcohol, or kill another animal; and that all animals are equal. The commandments are to be painted on the end wall of the barn, the pigs explain, and would be "an unalterable law" governing Animal Farm forever.[11]

The next big task is the hay harvest. But there is a slight hitch while the cows have to be milked by the pigs. The animals wonder what will be done with the milk. One of the hens remarks that when Mr. Jones ran things some of the milk was mixed with their food. Napoleon tells them not to worry about the milk but to attend to the harvest. By the evening the milk has disappeared.

The harvest goes well. The animals are happy and, despite having to find ways of adapting to tools meant for humans, the job goes smoothly. Each animal works according to its capacity. Boxer's strength and positive attitude are great assets. Because of their "superior knowledge," the pigs devote themselves to supervising rather than joining in the physical work.[12] Not everyone adapts easily to the new regime though. Mollie the mare does not always pull her weight, and neither does the cat. Benjamin the donkey continues as before, doing what he needs to do but without enthusiasm for the revolution.

Sunday is a rest day, and a time to meet around Animal Farm's new flag—a hoof and horn on a green field—and plan for the future. Meetings always end by singing "Beasts of England."

Napoleon and Snowball are starting to fall out, however. The other animals notice that the two pigs never agree in the meetings. Whatever suggestion one makes, the other opposes.

Despite the revolutionary spirit, it is clear that natural traits and tendencies mean there are still differences among the animals. The cat, for instance, cannot convince birds that she has suppressed her instinct to hunt them.

The ability to learn varies greatly too. While the pigs absorb crafts and skills quickly, other animals struggle with the alphabet. The sheep, hens, and ducks do not even manage to learn the Seven Commandments. To help them, Snowball creates a simple slogan which he says contains "the essential principle of Animalism." It is "Four legs good, two legs bad." He also has it painted on the wall above the commandments.

The sheep sometimes bleat the new slogan for hours on end. Perhaps Orwell had particular people in mind when he wrote about the sheep. One can speculate that thoughtless repetition of political doctrine would irritate him, and that he would want to make fun of people who vacantly bleated slogans.

In some of these details may be heard the voice of Eileen. According to friends, Orwell's wife had far more influence on the development of this story than on her husband's previous writings. She was said to be disappointed that she had not been consulted more in the past, and they attributed some of the sly digs in *Animal Farm* to her.[13]

While Snowball busies himself with slogans and other schemes, Napoleon concentrates on teaching a couple of litters of puppies. He takes them away from their mothers as soon as they are weaned, and keeps them so isolated that the rest of the animals soon forget them.

About this time the animals discover where the milk has been going. It is being added to the pigs' food, along with apples from the orchard. Milk and apples, Squealer explains, are essential for a pig's well-being. Do not imagine, he says, that the pigs are eating these choice foods "in a spirit of selfishness and privilege."[14] Many of them dislike milk and apples. They eat these things for the good of the farm, because if the pigs fail Mr. Jones will surely return. It is enough to convince the animals that the milk and apples should go to the pigs.

A TURNING POINT

In a letter written a few months after completing the book, Orwell described this milk-and-apples incident as the turning point in the story. The animals, he wrote, should not have allowed the pigs to start having special privileges because "there is no such thing as a benevolent dictatorship."[15]

News of the revolution on Animal Farm spread far beyond its boundaries. The neighboring two farmers, Mr. Pilkington and Mr. Frederick, become more hostile as the revolution prospers. But animals and birds everywhere are inspired, and "Beasts of England" is sung in fields and hedgerows despite protests and punishments from humans.

In October, after the harvest, there is a long-expected invasion by Mr. Jones and his men. Led by Snowball, the animals counterattack and drive the men off the farm. A new decoration is devised, Animal Hero, First Class, and awarded to Snowball and Boxer.

The humans do have one success, however. Shortly after the so-called Battle of the Cowshed with Mr. Jones, Mollie goes missing. Weeks later, pigeons report seeing her harnessed to a cart, wearing ribbons and contentedly eating sugar. Her defection is never mentioned by the animals again.

The pigs continue to expand their hold on the planning and leadership of the farm. Snowball and Napoleon still cannot agree about anything. Snowball's prize scheme is to build a windmill, which he claims can be used to provide electrical power and reduce the animals' workload. Napoleon, on the other hand, says it would be better to concentrate on increasing food production.

There is a dispute too about how to defend the farm against more human attacks. Snowball argues for spreading the revolution to other farms. The humans would have their hands full dealing with these new outbreaks, he reasons. Napoleon favors obtaining firearms and training themselves to fight. The animals listen to both sides but cannot agree what to do.

A meeting is held to decide whether to go ahead with building the windmill. Napoleon says the idea is nonsense, but Snowball is very persuasive. There is not much doubt that he will get his way until suddenly Napoleon utters a peculiar whimper. This is the signal for nine enormous dogs to bound into the barn and attack Snowball, who only just manages to escape. The dogs are the puppies Napoleon has been raising, and they chase Snowball off the farm. (This parallels the exile of Trotsky in 1929 after a power struggle with Stalin. Trotsky eventually sought refuge in Mexico City, where he was assassinated by a Stalinist agent in 1940.)

The animals are terrified, and dismayed too when they are told that there will be no more Sunday morning debates. In the future, a committee of pigs, with Napoleon in charge, will make decisions about the running of the farm. Almost immediately Squealer begins to build up Napoleon's reputation as a self-sacrificing leader and to condemn Snowball as "no better than a criminal." (Again, this reflects what happened in Russia. To orthodox Communists, Trotsky became a scapegoat. As Orwell experienced in Spain, anyone who differed with official Stalinist policy was in danger of being branded a Trotskyist.)

Napoleon's decisions, like Stalin's, can appear to be extraordinary flip-flops. It takes a skilled propagandist such as Squealer to explain away the contradictions. For instance, Squealer soon announces that the windmill had been Napoleon's idea all along. Then Napoleon decides to trade, and even form alliances, with the neighboring farms. Napoleon's relations with his neighbors,

Mr. Pilkington and Mr. Frederick, are just as unstable as those that inspired Orwell's fable. (Again, there is a parallel with real events. Stalin made a nonagression pact with Hitler that was only broken when the Nazis invaded the Soviet Union after the start of World War II. Suddenly Germany and Russia went from being friends to enemies. Stalin needed a new alliance, this time with the Western democracies, Britain and the United States.)

Sometimes new developments seem to go against the Seven Commandments, such as when the pigs start sleeping in the beds in the farmhouse. But when the animals go to the barn to read the commandments on the wall, they find there are changes in the wording. The commandment prohibiting sleeping in beds now merely bans sleeping in a bed with sheets.

Morale among the animals is hurt further when several pigs, sheep, hens, and a goose confess that they were conspiring with Snowball. Much to the shock of most of the animals, the dogs kill those who confess on the spot. To console themselves, the other animals sing "Beasts of England." Then Squealer announces that the song is "no longer needed" now that the revolution has been accomplished. It is now forbidden to sing it.

Another attack by humans has been expected. This time it is Mr. Frederick of Pinchfield Farm who invades. The battle does not go well for the animals. The humans blow up the recently completed windmill. Indignant at this, the animals charge forward and after a hard-fought struggle they win back the ground they had lost and the humans run away.

Winter arrives and, with more mouths to feed, conditions are harsh. But few have long enough memories to make comparisons with life under Mr. Jones. So it comes as no surprise that when an election is held for president of Animal Farm, Napoleon is the only candidate.

Napoleon's most loyal supporter, other than the dogs and Squealer, has been Boxer. But the cart horse is growing old and his strength is not what it was. When he collapses, Boxer must be treated by a vet in a nearby town, Squealer says. A horse-drawn van arrives at the farm to transport him. Only the urgent protests of Benjamin the donkey alert the animals to the name of a slaughterhouse written on the side of the van. Boxer is being sent to be killed, Benjamin tells them, but it is too late. The van leaves before Boxer can be freed. Of course, Squealer has an explanation: The vet had bought the used van and had not yet painted out the old lettering. The animals are urged to follow Boxer's example of loyalty and hard work.

In the coming years, the farm prospers. The windmill is rebuilt. But the better living standards Snowball had predicted do not come about, except for the pigs and the dogs. "The truest happiness," Napoleon says, lies in "working hard and living frugally."

One evening the animals are astonished to see Squealer on his hind legs. Other pigs emerge from the farmhouse walking in the same way. Finally, Napoleon appears, standing upright with a whip grasped in his

Chinese actors are pictured here performing in a stage version of Orwell's *Animal Farm* performed in Beijing on November 21, 2002.

trotter and the dogs by his side. On cue, just as they had been trained to do, the sheep bleat a new slogan: "Four legs good, two legs better."[16]

Clover and Benjamin go to the barn to consult the Seven Commandments. But there is now only a single commandment painted on the wall, a new one that reads: "All animals are equal but some animals are more equal than others."[17]

A week later, the animals are weeding a turnip field when several neighboring farmers arrive at the farmhouse. They had been invited for a tour of the farm. The animals creep up to a window and watch as pigs and humans drink beer and play cards. Mr. Pilkington gives a toast in which he says that he and his friends no longer feel threatened by pigs running a farm. The up-to-date methods, discipline, and orderliness they have seen during their tour set an example for them all. The "lower" animals on Animal Farm, he says, do more work and receive less food than any other animals in the county.

In reply, Napoleon sets aside what little is left of Animal Farm's revolutionary principles. Normal business relations with their neighbors is their aim, he says. The rumors that they want to stir up rebellion on neighboring farms could not be further from the truth. In the future, he adds, the old custom among the animals of addressing each other as "comrade" is to be suppressed, and the hoof and horn on the farm's green flag are to be removed. Finally, the name of the farm is to be changed back to Manor Farm.

The card game resumes, only for a quarrel to break out when Napoleon and Mr. Pilkington both play an ace of spades simultaneously. The animals outside compare the faces of the humans and the pigs, "but already it was impossible to say which was which."[18]

TRAVELS AND TRAGEDY

With *Animal Farm* at the publisher, Orwell had one final chance to play a role in wartime events. He was offered a position as a foreign correspondent for a British newspaper, the *Observer*. He accepted and went to Paris in February 1945 to report on post-Nazi Europe.

Perhaps the most noteworthy incident during this trip was a brief meeting with Ernest Hemingway, from whom Orwell reportedly borrowed a pistol because he was afraid he might be attacked by communist agents.[19]

Orwell was far more vulnerable, it turned out, because of his poor health. His illness at this time, probably related to his weak lungs, was serious enough for him to write instructions about which of his books he wanted to remain in print after his death. He rejected two of his novels on this score, *A Clergyman's Daughter* and *Keep the Aspidistra Flying*, which he described as "silly pot-boilers."[20]

Then came news about Eileen. She had gone into the hospital in England for what they both assumed to be a routine operation. Tumors on her uterus required a hysterectomy to avoid the risk of cancer. Whether Eileen fully communicated with her husband about her condition is debated by his biographers.[21] At any rate, there was apparently no reason to think she would be in serious danger during the operation. However, while in surgery, Eileen had a reaction to the anesthetic and died of heart failure.[22]

After a brief stay in England for the funeral and to make arrangements for his son Richard's care, Orwell returned to Europe to continue reporting on post-war Germany. Perhaps by immersing himself in his job as a correspondent, he might be better able to deal with the shock of Eileen's death.[23]

A FOCUS ON ESSAYS

Even when he finished his reporting assignment in Germany, Orwell continued to commit himself to work. His output of essays increased greatly during the years 1945 and 1946. The range of topics he tackled was impressive. Politics and literature were included, of course. But he also veered away from his main preoccupations to write about other subjects, such as how to make a good cup of tea and Spanish surrealist painter Salvador Dali—concluding that one can dislike a man and still appreciate his artistic talent.

Despite detesting Nazism, he had no heart for the persecution of the defeated Germans that he saw as a war correspondent, and said as much in an essay entitled "Revenge Is Sour." A related sentiment is evident in "Notes On Nationalism," an opinion piece in which he contrasts patriotism—defined as "devotion to a particular place and a particular way of life, which one believes to be the best in the world but has no wish to force on other people"—with the blind promotion of a place or idea.[24] The latter he associated with the concept of nationalism.

At times he could be lighthearted, even though he almost invariably had a serious point to make. "Some Thoughts on the Common Toad," for instance, may be a celebration of spring but it also expresses relief that seasonal cycles were still beyond the power of bureaucrats and dictators.

Another essay, "Riding Down from Bangor," is devoted to the American literature that was part of

Orwell's childhood reading. He had formed his first impressions of the United States from such books as *Tom Sawyer, Uncle Tom's Cabin* and *Little Women*. He had been drawn, he wrote, to the innocence and gaiety of American life in the nineteenth century as expressed in its literature. He was not so complimentary about the American popular culture of his own day, however. His topic is all the more interesting because Orwell has been accused of ignoring the importance of the United States in his work.[25] Clearly, he respected the literature of the country though. Among his essay subjects are the American writers Mark Twain and Jack London. In fact, most of the best writers in English of the era following World War I were Irish or American, he commented.[26]

The essay from this period that perhaps has attracted the most attention is "Politics and the English Language." It gives instructions on how to use language clearly. Start by deciding what you mean to say, Orwell wrote, and take care to use appropriate words and avoid overused phrases and metaphors. Among the worst abusers of the English language, claimed Orwell, are academics and politicians.

There is also a foretaste in the essay of a central idea in Newspeak, the language form Orwell devised for his final novel, *1984*. Slovenly language, he wrote in the essay, can make it easier for us to have foolish thoughts. In a comparable link between words and their effect, Newspeak's skillfully manipulated vocabulary limits people's capacity to think.

ISLAND LIVING

A year after his wife's death, Orwell was still living in the London apartment they had shared. His routine seems to have varied little, consisting mainly of writing articles and essays, meeting literary colleagues for meals or drinks, and looking after his son Richard. His parental duties were shared with a housekeeper.

Before Eileen's death, the couple had been planning a holiday on the remote island of Jura, off the west coast of Scotland. The destination had been suggested by David Astor, owner of the *Observer* newspaper, for which Orwell had been writing articles and reviews. They had been offered the use of an empty farmhouse called Barnhill. Rather than a holiday, though, Orwell and his wife considered the prospect of making Barnhill their home.

Finally, in mid-1946, Orwell was ready to act upon the Barnhill plan. Not only would the move free him from the pressures of the literary life in London, but also he felt Jura would be a fine place for Richard to spend his childhood. The housekeeper moved with them, but she soon returned south when Orwell's younger sister Avril took over the role of looking after Richard.

It was in these surroundings, which many might find bleak and lonely, that Orwell wrote most of *1984*.

THE YEAR
OF DYSTOPIA

Examining *1984*

At first, Orwell's last novel, *1984*, might appear to be a work of political prophesy, and one that turned out to be wrong. After all, the year in which it is set is history now, and the specific circumstances Orwell described when he was writing in the late 1940s did not come to pass. Britain was not renamed Airstrip One and did not become part of a huge superpower called Oceania which also included North and South America.

In the era leading up to 1984, the title of the book caused some people to expect it to be a cataclysmic year. But Orwell himself did not mean the year in the title to be taken literally. He wrote much of the book in 1948, and it is easy to see how he might have reversed the last two numerals to represent an arbitrary year which was then far in the future. Even when the book was nearing publication, Orwell and his British publisher were still considering *The Last Man in Europe* as an alternative title.[1]

Orwell's intended target, he explained, was the totalitarianism that was so much a part of the communist and fascist regimes of Europe. He made it clear though that he still believed in socialism as the best political model.[2]

Several influences evidently went into the making of the novel. Orwell's memories of school days and of policing in Burma must have affected his view of authority and how it is imposed. Among the writers who likely influenced his thinking is Arthur Koestler, whose 1941 novel *Darkness at Noon* is also about a struggle between the individual and a totalitarian system. The two writers crossed paths in London literary circles and Orwell devoted an essay to Koestler's work. Also, Orwell's former French teacher Aldous Huxley had written his own version of a utopia gone wrong. (Huxley's *Brave New World* was published in 1932.)

An intriguing possibility is that Orwell took his title, perhaps subconsciously, from a poem his wife Eileen had written while she was in school. It was entitled "End of the Century, 1984" and seems to have been inspired by Huxley's novel. It is not known for certain if Orwell read the poem.[3]

DYSTOPIA—*An imagined world in which authorities have turned people's lives into a nightmare of restrictions and prohibitions.*

THE WORLD OF *1984*

Like *Animal Farm, 1984* is not just relevant to one period or one place. The ideas Orwell expressed through his story can be applied in a far wider context. In essence, the book is about the pressure on the individual to conform—a central theme, in Orwell's work as his previous books show. A combination of totalitarian ideology and pervasive technology can make that situation all the more terrifying, of course, and the novel does draw much of its impact from that uniquely modern circumstance.

Taken to the extremes described in *1984*, the pressure to conform is applied through various forms of oppression. Ultimately the individual must submit completely to the will of those in charge. That means not just obeying but being totally devoted to the rulers. The grim world described by Orwell is called a dystopia, as opposed to the ideal conditions of a utopia.

Headed by a mysterious leader called Big Brother, the Party controlling Oceania manipulates virtually every aspect of Party members' lives. Only Party members are important. Most of the population consists of proles— short for the proletariat, or lower classes. The Party considers the proles to be incapable of doing much of anything. They absorb the entertainment the Party provides, generally work at insignificant jobs, and are expected to show loyalty to the Party. They are not expected to take any initiative. For many, taking part in Oceania's lottery is the main reason for living.

Events such as Hate Week and the daily Two Minutes Hate give everyone a chance to shout insults at pictures of the enemies of the state. Chief among these is Emmanuel Goldstein, who was once a Party leader and is now considered a traitor.

As a reminder that Oceania is perpetually at war, several bombs fall on London each week. Like the rockets that hit England during World War II, they fall out of the sky with little warning, destroying homes and killing civilians at random.

As Orwell was writing in the mid-twentieth century, it is natural to think of fascism and communism when reading *1984*. Orwell even had one of his characters mention these political systems as precedents for the Party that controls everything in the story. But he also took ideas from earlier periods, and would surely have had no trouble finding more material in the world since *1984*.

One recurring idea in the story, for example, is that there are cameras and microphones recording everything the central characters do and say. Orwell described something he called a telescreen, which is like a television except that, besides broadcasting propaganda, it also records everything going on within view of its screen.

While telescreens are not with us yet, we have become accustomed to electronic surveillance in other forms. Security cameras record our activities at airports, stores, public events, and even on the streets. Cell phones can pinpoint our locations. Computers track our interests and searches for information. Police helicopters and military satellites have the ability to observe us to an extent that even Orwell could not have anticipated.

THE PARTY'S CONTROL OF LANGUAGE AND IDEAS

The impact *1984* has had is evident in the extent its ideas have become part of Western culture. Some of the words and expressions Orwell coined are now in widespread use.

The ruling party in the story is in the process of revising and updating the English language. In some cases, words are being eliminated or their meanings restricted. If people's vocabulary can be controlled, then so can their thoughts. The new version of English is called Newspeak.

THOUGHT CRIME— *A term created by Orwell for* 1984 *to describe thoughts that the party considered to be wrong.*

A couple of its more important terms are "doublethink," meaning primarily the ability to believe two contradictory ideas at the same time, and "thought crime," the notion that thinking the wrong thing can be a crime in itself. Another recurring term is Ingsoc, which in Oldspeak would have been "English Socialism."

Even the title of the book now prompts visions of an evil dictatorship in which individuals have no freedom. The term "Orwellian" has similar associations. And, of course, Big Brother has become universally recognized as the figurehead of totalitarianism.

Above all, *1984* is a story about ideas and their consequences. The sequence of events is limited. There is relatively little action in the novel, and not that many characters involved. The focus is on three central characters—Winston Smith, Julia, and O'Brien—and the role they play in the struggle against Oceania's political system. Minor players serve to intensify that focus rather than having subplots of their own. They function to a large extent to illustrate how the political system works.

Protagonist Winston Smith is already straying from approved behavior as *1984* begins. He has bought a blank book and, out of sight of the telescreen in his London flat, starts to write a diary. Making private observations is not illegal, but would not be tolerated for long if it were known. A branch of government called the Thought Police tracks down those with independent ideas.

Winston is a Party member and works for the Ministry of Truth. His job brings to mind the wartime occupations of Orwell as a radio propagandist and his wife Eileen as a censor. Winston rewrites old newspapers and books to reflect the government's current version of the facts. For example, Oceania suddenly changes its relationship with the other two superpowers that dominate the world, Eurasia and Eastasia. Its former ally, Eastasia, becomes the enemy and Eurasia is now a friend. Winston has to erase all references to the war that was being fought with Eurasia. The official position is that it never happened and Oceania has always been at war with Eastasia.

Sometimes people are arrested for political crimes and disappear. One of Winston's tasks is to eliminate all references to those people, so that there is no evidence they existed. In these ways, history is continually being rewritten. This reflects the Party slogan—Who controls the past controls the future: who controls the present controls the past. In writing this, Orwell may have had in mind his exasperation at press coverage of the war in Spain a decade earlier.

There are brief descriptions of a couple of Winston's colleagues at the Ministry of Truth. One of them, Parsons, also lives in the same block of flats. He and his wife have a nine-year-old son and seven-year-old daughter who are devoted to the Party and belong to a youth organization called the Spies. Children are among the Party's most ferocious supporters. It is common to hear of them reporting their parents to the Thought Police for political crimes, and no one looks forward to the periodic public hanging of prisoners of war with more eagerness.

JULIA AND O'BRIEN

Two people with whom Winston works are to have a special importance for him. A young woman named Julia becomes his lover. They meet in secret, at first in solitary places in the countryside and then in a rented room in a district inhabited by proles. The room is above a junk shop where Winston bought the book he is using as his diary. He likes the old objects in the shop, and the room has a feeling of home about it that his flat lacks. The location was not chosen randomly. Orwell wrote on more than one occasion of his pleasure at uncovering bargains in London's secondhand shops.

O'Brien is a senior member of the Party, and seems an unlikely ally for Winston. But Winston senses that O'Brien shares his thoughts about the evil of the system under which they live. Winston is sure he is not alone in feeling oppressed. It is rumored that there is a secretive organization called the Brotherhood which opposes the government.

Winston and Julia become friends after she hands

him a note saying she loves him. It is a surprise to Winston, who had been thinking that she was spying on him for the Party. They arrange a secret meeting in the country. Becoming lovers is itself a politically dangerous act. The Party only approves of such relationships for the purpose of producing children within marriage. Other than that, Party members are discouraged from having sexual or romantic relationships.

Winston already has a wife, Katherine, but she is too much of an orthodox thinker for his liking and they separated long ago. Julia, on the other hand, is a rebel who eagerly embraces emotional and physical passion. Their lovemaking seems to Winston to be "a blow struck against the Party." Sooner or later, they are both convinced, the Thought Police will catch them. But, Winston says, "some kinds of failure are better than other kinds."[4]

As suggested earlier, story development in *1984* often takes a backseat to the ideas and concepts Orwell wanted to express. Another writer might have introduced more suspense as the relationship between Winston and Julia began. Orwell opted to be direct and simple in his narrative. For example, the love note Julia hands to Winston serves to introduce them to each other but is perhaps too much of a convenient device to be convincing. As portrayed by Orwell, Julia makes up her mind about people quickly. All the same, her approach to Winston may strike readers as improbably reckless.

In portraying Julia, Orwell may have used his soon-to-be second wife, Sonia Brownell, as a model. The couple met through a literary magazine, *Horizon*, where Brownell worked as an assistant to Orwell's friend Cyril Connolly. Both women, the fictitious and the real, shared a forthright and independent spirit, and Brownell's friends had no doubt of her role as a blueprint for Julia.[5]

While Winston dreams of overthrowing the system, Julia only wants to deceive the authorities. On the surface she's a loyal follower of the Party. She does not believe in the propaganda, but has no hope of political change.

O'Brien is more likely a link to the Party's opposition. Despite O'Brien's high ranking in the Party, Winston feels that he is a kindred spirit. Once Winston had dreamed of an unseen person saying: "We shall meet in the place where there is no darkness."[6] The voice, he was convinced, belonged to O'Brien.

The two men finally talk after encountering each other in a corridor at the Ministry of Truth. O'Brien offers to give Winston an advance copy of the latest Newspeak dictionary. The book, O'Brien says, is at his flat. He gives Winston the address and suggests he come by for it. Winston assumes the dictionary is just an excuse for a further meeting. He arrives with Julia at O'Brien's flat ready to join the Brotherhood.

After turning off the telescreen in the room—a privilege given to senior Party members—O'Brien confirms the existence of the Brotherhood and Emmanuel Goldstein. As might be expected from a revolutionary movement, the Brotherhood operates in small groups. Individuals know only their immediate contacts.

Julia and Winston promise to do virtually anything for the cause—except give up their relationship. They tell O'Brien about their hiding place at the junk shop, and O'Brien promises to give Winston a book written by Goldstein explaining the world in which they live.

GOLDSTEIN'S BOOK

Lengthy passages of Goldstein's book make up *1984*. At one point, Orwell had to resist suggestions that this section should be cut from the American edition. It remains a hard section to digest for some readers, but Orwell clearly felt the information was essential to understanding his story.

The Goldstein book has chapters analyzing the Party's strategies and slogans, which include "Ignorance Is Strength" and "War Is Peace." Although these seem like products of doublethink, the book is able to show a degree of logic in them.

The object of continual warfare is not to conquer and defeat the other superpowers but to maintain the existing social and political order within Oceania. War provides an outlet for material resources and builds support for the political hierarchy. The resulting stability, according to this view, makes war comparable to peace.

People have always been divided into three social and political strata, the Goldstein book explains. The High consists of the rulers, whose aim is to maintain their power. The Middle struggles to replace the High. The Low would like a society in which all men are equal. For the most part though, people in the Low category are too preoccupied by the drudgery and servitude of their daily lives to do much about it.

Since coming to power in the mid-twentieth century, the Party has worked to keep this hierarchy static. The proles, representing the Low, are not considered a threat. The outer Party members, representing the Middle, are the ones to watch.

Apart from the constant surveillance, certain measures have helped suppress opposition. To begin with, private property was put into public ownership. In effect, that meant that the Party controlled virtually all Oceania's resources, be they industrial, technological, intellectual, or artistic. Furthermore, it is hard to find a target for rebellion. Oceania has no capital and the whereabouts—even the existence—of Big Brother is a mystery, despite his poster on display everywhere. Overall, keeping the population ignorant about the reality of their circumstances keeps the Party strong. If the population supports that policy, all the better.

BETRAYAL AND ARREST

As Winston and Julia fear, they are tracked down and arrested. Winston finds himself in a windowless cell, presumably in the headquarters of the Ministry of Love, which is responsible for law and order. O'Brien enters the cell. At first Winston assumes he has been arrested too. It turns out O'Brien is there to interrogate him. Apparently Winston has been tricked. O'Brien is a Party man after all.

Under torture, Winston readily confesses to many things he did not do and agrees with things he knows to be untrue. It is not enough simply to give the right answers though. What is important, in the Party's view, is that Winston has complete belief in what the Party tells him. He must be punished until his will to resist is broken.

"We shall squeeze you empty," O'Brien tells him, "and then we shall fill you with ourselves."[7]

Perhaps worst of all, there will be no record of Winston's existence, let alone his ordeal. The Party has learned from repressive regimes of the past, such as the Catholic Church's Inquisition, the fascists, and communists. Their victims became martyrs. The Party leaves no evidence.

During Winston's indoctrination, O'Brien discusses various aspects of the Party's system of government. He even talks about Goldstein's book, which he claims to have had a share in writing. He asks what Winston thinks is the Party's ultimate motive. Winston anticipates the answer to be "the good of the majority." But O'Brien corrects him. The Party "seeks power entirely for its own sake," he says.[8]

He mentions another Party slogan: Freedom Is Slavery. Only by merging himself with the Party, O'Brien explains, can the individual be "all-powerful and immortal."[9]

The reader might wonder why O'Brien is taking such trouble to detail these ideas to a person who officially does not exist. In an explanation more evocative of religion than politics, O'Brien's comments that it is because "you are a flaw in the pattern, Winston. You are a stain that must be wiped out. . . . When finally you surrender to us, it must be of your own free will."[10]

Physically, Winston has been reduced to little more than a skeleton. He longs for the bullet in the back of the neck that is the typical end for political prisoners. To die hating his tormentors offers some consolation. Winston has to face one final source of terror though. He still hates Big Brother. O'Brien has to change that.

Winston is taken to Room 101, where prisoners face their worst fears. For each victim it is different. Winston's worst fear is rats. He is strapped to a chair in front of a cage containing two famished rodents. In the poorer areas of the city, O'Brien says, unattended babies are sometimes attacked by rats.

"They show astonishing intelligence in knowing when a human being is helpless," he adds.[11] O'Brien moves the cage in front of Winston's face. If he opens the cage door, he explains, the rats will have to bore through Winston's face in order to escape. In panic, Winston begs O'Brien to do it to Julia instead of him. The cage door stays closed. O'Brien has achieved his goal. Winston has even betrayed the woman he loves.

The Party releases Winston, and gives him a job too. But he is a broken man. He passes time drinking the Party's alcoholic staple, Victory Gin, in the Chestnut Tree Café.

There is a chance meeting with Julia. They admit that they have betrayed each other. Under torture they had each been reduced to trying to save themselves. After that, they agree, it would be impossible to revive their relationship.

As he drinks his gin at the café, there is a news flash from the telescreen. There has been an important battle against Eurasia, now the enemy again. Victory has been snatched from the jaws of defeat. On the wall is a portrait of Big Brother, the rock against which Oceania's enemies dash themselves in vain. At last Winston is ready for "the final, indispensable, healing change. . . . He had won the victory over himself. He loved Big Brother."[12]

NEWSPEAK

The book ends with an appendix about Newspeak. Orwell went into far more detail in this than is necessary for the story alone. From his essays, it is evident that he was fascinated by how language is used. At school, he apparently had a mixed record as a student of Latin and French. But living in Burma, Paris, and Spain had given him a familiarity with several languages.

While Orwell wrote news stories as a BBC radio producer during World War II, his wife Eileen worked as a government censor. Between the two of them they must have developed a subtle appreciation of how meaning can be shaped by language.[13]

Newspeak is split into an A vocabulary, for use in common, everyday situations, and a B vocabulary, which consists of specially coined political terms "intended to impose a desirable mental attitude upon the person using them."

Euphony, the sound of words, is an important way of reinforcing this state of mind. Newspeak aims for "a gabbling style of speech, at once staccato and monotonous."[14]

There is also a C vocabulary of technical and scientific terms. Newspeak is scheduled to completely replace Oldspeak by the year 2050. At that point, virtually anything written before about 1960 would be untranslatable.

BASIC ENGLISH

Orwell's job at the BBC left its mark on *1984* in several ways. Some of his ideas about terminology, language, procedure and locations apparently stem from his experiences as a producer, where he became acquainted with a concept called Basic English.

Devised before the war by British linguist C.K. Ogden, Basic English was a streamlined form of the language that was intended to make English a clearer and more universal medium. It had a core vocabulary of 850 words and eliminated jargon. The British government promoted Basic, and there were attempts to promote its use at the BBC.[15]

PUBLIC REACTION

Initial sales and reviews in Britain and the United States must have given Orwell some idea of the impact *1984* would have. Within a year, sales in Britain and the United States were more than 400,000 copies, according to biographers, and would increase to more than a million worldwide annually by the novel's namesake year of 1984.[16]

Reviewers on both sides of the Atlantic praised the book for the most part. The predictable exceptions were those writing for communist publications. As with *Animal Farm*, Orwell had to point out that his target was totalitarianism. He had not deserted socialism.

Apparently Orwell was pleased that some reviewers noted that *1984* differed from other utopian or dystopian novels. His book was intended as a warning of what could happen in the real world. As such, it built on ideology and policies that had already been evident in fascist and communist regimes. In this it contrasted with the general concept of a utopia as a fantasy or a set of circumstances removed from the real world.[17]

Since Orwell's death, *1984* has come to be regarded as one of the most important books of the past century. Translated into numerous languages, it has become a key work in understanding modern culture and politics.

THE IMPACT OF ORWELL

The Legacy of George Orwell

O rwell finished writing *1984* in late 1948. Apart from a handful of essays, his career was virtually at an end. The health problems that had plagued him since childhood were becoming more serious. His spartan life on Jura and the exertion of writing had worn him down. Once more his lungs were the main problem. He had been diagnosed with tuberculosis, and eventually this would be listed as his cause of death.[1]

Even while he was wasting away in those final months, Orwell did not entirely give up his dreams for the future. He still yearned to be in his island home. Instead, his illness meant he had to be a patient in the city of Glasgow and, finally, in a London hospital. He thought, too, of writing more fiction—he mentioned Burma as a setting for a short novel—but he was no longer up to the effort.[2]

He could still surprise friends, however. After Eileen's

death, he yearned for female companionship and, in desperation, proposed marriage to a couple of women he hardly knew. Finally, the bedridden Orwell received a positive response from *Horizon* magazine's girl Friday, Sonia Brownell. With Orwell's return to southern England from Jura, their friendship had revived and Sonia visited him while he was convalescing.

The reasons for their marriage, which took place on October 13, 1949, remain in dispute. Though fifteen years Orwell's junior, Sonia was well-known in the arts communities of London and Paris. Orwell could depend on her being a capable caretaker of his work after he died. For her part, Sonia has been described as a woman habitually drawn to creative talent in need of nurturing.

Biographers differ greatly about Sonia's personality and motives. It has been suggested that she had her eyes on the wealth that Orwell was beginning to acquire from book sales. Friends observed genuine affection between the two, though, and Sonia did indeed watch over her husband's legacy until her death in 1980.[3]

Orwell died on January 21, 1950, after a lung hemorrhaged. Sonia and he had been due to travel to a sanatorium in Switzerland three days later, where Orwell might have benefited from the climate.

Just as unexpected as his marriage was Orwell's request to be buried in a church cemetery, considering the atheistic leanings in his work. Perhaps he was attracted by the idea of a quintessential English resting place. Reportedly his friends had to search to find a clergyman who would accept the remains of a nonbeliever. His grave, marked with his name at birth, Eric Blair, is in the village of Sutton Courtenay, near Oxford.

ORWELL'S REPUTATION

Almost inevitably, the reputations of influential figures are affected by trends and revelations after their deaths. In Orwell's case, one such revelation was that he had compiled a list of names of possible communist spies and sympathizers among Britain's intelligentsia. Apparently, a few months before his death, he gave this list to a friend who worked for the Information Research Department (IRD), which was a part of the British Foreign Office.[4]

Critics in recent years have suggested that Orwell betrayed acquaintances by doing this. Apologists for him have argued that Orwell openly talked and wrote about who might cooperate with both the Soviets and the Nazis. Besides, they contend, the IRD had no legal power over anyone and Orwell was simply warning against the influence of totalitarian sympathizers.[5]

With such potential for controversy in mind perhaps, Orwell insisted that he did not want anyone to write a biography about him. Biography tended to be either inaccurate or humiliating, he felt, and besides he wanted the focus to be on his work rather than his life story.[6]

In 1960 Sonia established the Orwell Archive at University College London. With the help of archivist Ian Angus, she then compiled a four-volume set of Orwell's essays, articles and letters. When it was published in 1968, the set impressed reviewers with Orwell's abilities as a journalist. In remembering him for his novels, despite their inconsistencies—particularly in the early years—critics had tended to overlook his nonfiction.

Sonia came under pressure to authorize a biography—partly to head off unauthorized versions.[7] A political economist, Bernard Crick, was given the go-ahead. His book was eventually published in 1980, the same year Sonia died from cancer.

In the end, the Orwell legacy was a mixed blessing for Sonia. The collection of his essays and letters she had worked so hard to compile did indeed boost her husband's reputation. But she had less success with his business affairs, and died without much benefit from his considerable royalties.[8]

Fittingly, it was George and Eileen's son, Richard, who seems to have found the most lasting peace of mind. After the death of his adopted father, Richard remained in the care of his aunt Avril in Scotland. As an adult he would opt for a life far removed from literary circles, raising a family of his own and working for a company making agricultural equipment.[9]

ORWELL'S LEGACY

As George Orwell would have expected, his books have varied greatly in their impact since his death. It was his final two works of fiction, *Animal Farm* and *1984*, that ensured his fame. *Animal Farm* is widely considered the benchmark for modern political allegory. *1984*, with its instantly identifiable catchphrases, has become a vital reference for opposing authoritarian government.

Orwell's nonfiction is also still admired. The commentaries he based on his travels in Paris, London, Wigan, and Spain remain valued records of that era. His essays and book reviews have continued to impress readers with his insight and candor, particularly after his widow, Sonia, helped rejuvenate interest by republishing them in 1968.

As late as the early 1940s, however, Orwell's legacy was not assured. His fiction up to that point had received a mixed reception. His "dreary books" convinced one critic "that nature didn't intend him to be a novelist."[10] Orwell himself left instructions—subsequently disregarded— that a couple of his novels were not good enough to be republished after his death.

Even friends and colleagues disagreed, in retrospect, over what should be remembered about him. There were those who valued his ideas more than his talents as a writer, and those who singled out his literary style with "its firmness, its colloquial vigor, its unpretentious vividness, and, above all, its limpid clarity," as his fellow writer George Woodcock put it.[11]

A FINAL VIEW

For some of his acquaintances, Orwell's rapid rise in the world of literature in the mid-1940s was a surprise.

Canadian writer George Woodcock, who lived in London and knew Orwell, wrote about "the myth . . . of the tortured, tragic writer, who died in his prime after a life of heroic hardships." The myth turns Orwell into "a figure hardly recognizable by those who knew him," he added.[12]

In Orwell, Woodcock saw instead a modern Don Quixote, who like the hero in Cervantes' novel, was ever prepared to champion eccentric or minority causes.[13] To him, Orwell was a man willing to be outspoken about his convictions, and that is the impression that prevails. With time, the nature and importance of those convictions are not so easily recalled. The threat of a cold war apocalypse no longer generates fear, and Orwell's faith in socialism as the doctrine of the future seems dated.

Nonetheless, his name and works have become bywords against tyranny and political hypocrisy. Surely Orwell would have approved of that.

CHRONOLOGY

1903—Eric Arthur Blair is born on June 25 in Motihari, a village in Bengal, India.

1911—In September, begins first term as a boarder at St. Cyprian's preparatory school.

1917—In May, begins attending school at Eton on a scholarship.

1922—On October 27, leaves England to take up appointment with the Indian Imperial Police in Burma.

1927—Returns home on leave in August.

1928—On the first day of January, resigns from the Burmese police, having announced plans to devote himself to writing. Leaves England in the spring to live in Paris.

1933—The British publication of the autobiographical *Down and Out in Paris and London* establishes his credentials as a social and political commentator.

1934—His first novel, *Burmese Days*, loosely based on his experiences in the police, is published in the United States, and in Britain the following year.

1935—His second novel, *A Clergyman's Daughter*, is published.

1936—Orwell travels in northern England for two months to research his account of working class conditions, *The Road to Wigan Pier*; his third novel, *Keep the Aspidistra Flying*, is published in Britain.

June 9: Orwell marries Eileen O'Shaughnessy, in their new home village of Wallington, in the county of Hertfordshire.

1937—*The Road to Wigan Pier* is published in Britain followed by *Homage to Catalonia* (1938), Orwell's account of his experiences earlier that year in the Spanish Civil War. Although sales are slow, the books reinforce his reputation as a political and social analyst.

1938—Accompanied by his wife, Eileen, goes to Morocco for several months to recuperate from illness.

1939—His novel, *Coming Up for Air*, is published in June in Britain, its narrative containing gloomy predictions about the world war Europe was about to enter.

1940—The collection of essays, *Inside the Whale*, is published.

1941—His essay "The Lion and the Unicorn" sets out his vision of Britain's political future as a socialist state. In August he starts work as a radio producer for the British Broadcasting Corporation's Empire Department, remaining in that job until September 1943.

1944—George and Eileen Orwell adopt a son, Richard Horatio.

1945—In March, Eileen dies in surgery while undergoing a hysterectomy. *Animal Farm*, his satire of Stalinist Russia, is published in August in Britain, and the following year in the United States.

1946—Moves to the Scottish island of Jura, where he writes his last book, *1984*.

1949—In June, *1984* is published. Marries Sonia Brownell in October.

1950—Orwell dies January 21 in London, at age forty-six.

1980—Orwell's second wife, Sonia, dies in London, at age sixty-two.

CHAPTER NOTES

CHAPTER 1. THE LIFE OF A WRITER

1. George Orwell, "Why I Write," *A Collection of Essays* (San Diego and New York: Harvest, 1981), p. 309.

2. Ibid., p. 309.

3. Ibid., p. 311.

4. Ibid., p. 312.

5. Ibid., p. 316.

6. Ibid., p. 316.

7. George Orwell, "Politics and the English Language," *A Collection of Essays* (San Diego and New York: Harvest, 1981), p. 156.

8. Michael Shelden, *Orwell: The Authorized Biography* (London: Heinemann; New York: HarperCollins, 1991), p. 487.

9. Bernard Crick, *George Orwell—A Life* (London: Secker and Warburg; Boston: Little, Brown and Company, 1980), p. 216. Also D. J. Taylor, *Orwell The Life* (London: Chatto & Windus; New York: Henry Holt, 2003), p. 143.

10. Gordon Bowker, *Inside George Orwell—A Biography* (London: Little, Brown; New York: Palgrave Macmillan, 2003), p. 430.

11. Ibid., p. 431.

12. George Orwell, *Orwell—My Country Right or Left: The Collected Essays, Journalism & Letters, Volume 2* (Nonpareil Books, 2000), p. 24.

13. Bowker, p. 394. Also Shelden, p. 429.

14. George Orwell, "Why I Write," *A Collection of Essays* (San Diego and New York: Harvest, 1981), p. 313.

15. George Orwell, "Charles Dickens," *A Collection of Essays* (San Diego and New York: Harvest, 1981), p. 96.

16. Ibid., p. 81.

17. George Orwell, "Inside the Whale," *A Collection of Essays* (San Diego and New York: Harvest, 1981), p. 221.

18. Ibid., p. 237.

CHAPTER 2. HIS LIFE AND WORK

1. George Orwell, "Such, Such Were the Joys," from *A Collection of Essays* (San Diego and New York: Harvest 1981), p. 37.

2. George Orwell, "Why I Write," from *A Collection of Essays* (San Diego and New York: Harvest 1981), p. 309.

3. "Such, Such Were the Joys," p. 21.

4. Ibid., p. 23.

5. George Orwell, *Orwell—An Age Like This: The Collected Essays, Journalism & Letters, Volume 1* (Nonpareil Books, 2000), p. 113.

6. George Woodcock, *The Crystal Spirit—A Study of George Orwell* (Schocken, originally published in 1966, new edition 1984; London: Jonathan Cape, 1969), p. 3.

7. George Orwell, *Homage to Catalonia* (San Diego, New York, London: Harvest 1952), p. 4.

CHAPTER 3. PAYING DUES

1. George Orwell, "Why I Write," from *A Collection of Essays* (San Diego, New York, London: Harvest, 1981), p. 309.

2. Michael Shelden, *Orwell: The Authorized Biography* (London: Heinemann; New York: HarperCollins, 1991), p. 128.

3. Ibid., p. 112.

4. Ibid., p. 134.

5. Ibid., p. 11. Also Gordon Bowker, *Inside George Orwell—A Biography* (London: Little, Brown; New York: Palgrave Macmillan, 2003), p. 98.

6. D. J. Taylor, *Orwell: The Life* (London: Chatto & Windus; New York: Henry Holt, 2003), p. 71.

7. Shelden, p. 140.

8. Ibid., p. 140.

9. Ibid., p. 142.

10. Ibid., p. 144.

11. Comparable accounts written nearer to Orwell's own time include *The Autobiography of a Super-tramp* by the poet W. H. Davies (1908) and *The People of the Abyss* (1903), in which American author Jack London delved into conditions in London's East End. Interestingly, Jack London—like Orwell after him—supplemented his experience of the slums by working in the hop fields of Kent, a common seasonal occupation for East Enders.

12. Shelden, p. 179.

13. George Orwell, *Orwell—An Age Like This: The Collected Essays, Journalism & Letters, Volume 1* (Nonpareil Books, 2000), p. 113.

14. Shelden, p. 150.

15. Ibid., pp. 194 and 182.

16. Ibid., p. 155. Also Orwell, p. 114.

17. George Orwell, *Down and Out in Paris and London* (San Diego, New York, London: Harvest, 1981), p. 51.

18. Ibid., p. 112.

19. Ibid., p. 7.

20. Ibid., p. 10.

21. Ibid., p. 38.

22. Ibid., p. 82.

23. Ibid., p. 91.

24. Ibid., p. 91.

25. Ibid., p. 115.

26. Ibid., p. 120.

27. Ibid., p. 121.

28. Ibid., p. 129.

29. Ibid., p. 134.

30. Ibid., p. 143.

31. Ibid., pp. 151 and 153.

32. Ibid., p. 167.

33. Ibid., p. 174.

34. Ibid., p. 203.

35. Ibid., p. 208.

36. Ibid., p. 213.

CHAPTER 4. REFLECTIONS ON BURMA

1. Michael Shelden, *Orwell: The Authorized Biography* (London: Heinemann; New York: HarperCollins, 1991), p. 155.

2. Ibid., p. 196.

3. Ibid., p. 165.

4. Ibid., p. 157.

5. Ibid., p. 195.

6. George Orwell, *Orwell—An Age Like This: The Collected Essays, Journalism & Letters, Volume 1* (Nonpareil Books, 2000), p. 115.

7. Bernard Crick, *George Orwell—A Life* (London: Secker and Warburg; Boston: Little, Brown and Company, 1980), p. 118.

8. Ibid., p. 82.

9. George Orwell, *Burmese Days* (San Diego, New York, London: Harvest, 1981), p. 69.

10. Shelden, p. 215.

11. Crick, p. 156. Also Shelden, p. 216.

12. Shelden, p. 221.

13. Ibid., p. 168.

14. Gordon Bowker, *Inside George Orwell—A Biography* (London: Little, Brown; New York: Palgrave Macmillan, 2003), p. 165.

15. Shelden, pp. 75 and 96.

16. Ibid., p. 117.

17. Ibid., p. 191.

18. Ibid., p. 245.

19. Ibid., pp. 223 and 246. Also Bowker, pp. 165 and 159.

20. George Orwell, *A Clergyman's Daughter* (San Diego, New York, London: Harvest, 1981), p. 11.

21. Ibid., p. 22.

22. Shelden, pp. 223 and 246. Also Bowker, pp. 165 and 159.

23. Crick, p. 165.

24. George Orwell, *Keep The Aspidistra Flying* (New York: Harbrace, 1993), p. 93.

25. Ibid., p. 37.

26. Ibid., p. 146.

27. Ibid., p. 41.

28. Ibid., p. 6.

29. Ibid., p. 238.

30. Ibid., p. 10.

31. Ibid., p. 72.

32. Bowker, p. 169.

33. Shelden, p. 255.

34. Ibid., p 246. Also Crick, p. 172.

CHAPTER 5. SETTING COURSE FOR WIGAN

1. D. J. Taylor, *Orwell: The Life* (New York: Henry Holt, 2003), p. 173.

2. Michael Shelden, *Orwell: The Authorized Biography* (New York: HarperCollins, 1991), p. 265.

3. Taylor, p. 167. Also Bernard Crick, *George Orwell—A Life* (Boston: Little, Brown and Company, 1980), p. 181.

4. Gordon Bowker, *Inside George Orwell—A Biography* (New York: Palgrave Macmillan, 2003), p. 180.

5. Ibid., p. 185.

6. George Orwell, *The Road to Wigan Pier* (New York, Berkley: Medallion, 1997), p. 120.

7. Ibid.

8. Ibid., p. 128.

9. Ibid., p. 144.

10. George Orwell, "Inside the Whale," *George Orwell: A Collection of Essays* (San Diego and New York: Harvest, 1981), p. 233.

11. Orwell, *The Road to Wigan Pier,* p. xvi.

12. Geoffrey Shryhane, *Peering At Wigan.* Self published and now out of print.

13. Ibid.

14. George Orwell, *The Road to Wigan Pier,* p. 21.

15. Ibid., p. 29.

16. Ibid., p. 31.

17. Ibid., p. 51.

18. Ibid., p. 78.

19. Ibid., p. 81.

20. Ibid., p. 84.

21. Ibid., p. 88.

22. Ibid., p. 79.

23. *Orwell Remembered,* ed. Audrey Coppard and Bernard Crick (New York: Facts on File, 1984), p. 133.

24. Orwell, *The Road to Wigan Pier,* p. 97.

25. Ibid., p. 134.

26. Ibid.

27. Shelden, p. 286.

28. Ibid., p. 270.

CHAPTER 6. WAR IN EUROPE

1. George Orwell, *Homage to Catalonia* (San Diego, New York, London: Harvest, 1981), p. 48.

2. Bernard Crick, *George Orwell—A Life* (Boston: Little, Brown And Company, 1980), p. 210.

3. George Orwell, *Homage to Catalonia* (San Diego, New York, London: Harvest, 1981), p. 5.

4. Ibid., p. 5.

5. Ibid., p. 13.

6. Ibid., p. 17.

7. Ibid., p. 40.

8. Ibid., p. 61.

9. Ibid., p. 105.

10. Ibid., p. 150.

11. Ibid., p. 181.

12. Ibid., p. 185.

13. Ibid., p. 223.

14. Ibid., p. 230.

15. Ibid., p. 231.

16. Ibid., p. 232.

17. Crick, p. 227.

18. Ibid., p. 211.

19. D. J. Taylor, *Orwell: The Life* (London: Chatto & Windus; New York: Henry Holt, 2003) p 252. Also Shelden, p. 349.

20. Michael Shelden, *Orwell: The Authorized Biography* (New York: HarperCollins, 1991), p. 340.

21. "Looking Back on the Spanish War," *George Orwell: A Collection of Essays* (San Diego and New York: Harvest, 1981), p. 199.

22. Ibid., p. 202.

23. Ibid., p. 210.

24. Michael Shelden, *Orwell: The Authorized Biography* (London: Heinemann; New York: HarperCollins, 1991), p. 345.

25. *Orwell—An Age Like This: The Collected Essays, Journalism & Letters, Volume 1* (Nonpareil Books, 2000), p. 344.

26. Ibid., pp. 353 and 360.

27. Gordon Bowker, *Inside George Orwell—A Biography* (London: Little, Brown; New York: Palgrave Macmillan, 2003), p. 251.

28. Bernard Crick, *George Orwell—A Life* (London: Secker and Warburg; Boston: Little, Brown and Company, 1980), p. 255.

29. George Orwell, *Coming Up for Air* (San Diego, New York, London: Harvest, 1981), p. 9.

30. Ibid., p. 28.

31. Ibid., p. 270.

32. Crick, p. 254.

33. Ibid., p. 262. Also Michael Shelden, *Orwell: The Authorized Biography* (London: Heinemann; New York: HarperCollins, 1991), p 378.

34. Bernard Crick, *George Orwell—A Life* (London: Secker and Warburg; Boston: Little, Brown and Company, 1980), p. 260. See also Michael Shelden, *Orwell: The Authorized Biography* (London: Heinemann; New York: HarperCollins, 1991), p. 377.

35. Gordon Bowker, *Inside George Orwell—A Biography*, (London: Little, Brown; New York: Palgrave Macmillan, 2003), p. 275.

36. Michael Shelden, *Orwell: The Authorized Biography* (London: Heinemann; New York: HarperCollins, 1991), p. 405.

37. Ibid., p. 394.

38. *Orwell—An Age Like This: The Collected Essays, Journalism & Letters, Volume 1* (Nonpareil Books, 2000), p. xix.

39. Bernard Crick, *George Orwell—A Life* (London: Secker and Warburg; Boston: Little, Brown and Company, 1980), p. 293.

40. Michael Shelden, *Orwell: The Authorized Biography* (London: Heinemann; New York: HarperCollins, 1991), p. 417.

41. Crick, p. 308.

42. Michael Shelden, *Orwell: The Authorized Biography* (London: Heinemann; New York: HarperCollins, 1991), p. 434.

43. Bernard Crick, *George Orwell—A Life* (London: Secker and Warburg; Boston: Little, Brown And Company, 1980), pp. 314–315.

CHAPTER 7. A POLITICAL FABLE

1. Michael Shelden, *Orwell: The Authorized Biography* (London: Heinemann; New York: HarperCollins, 1991), p. 444.

2. Bernard Crick, *George Orwell—A Life* (London: Secker and Warburg; Boston: Little, Brown and Company, 1980), p. 309. Also D. J. Taylor, *Orwell: The Life*, (London: Chatto & Windus; New York: Henry Holt, 2003), p. 322.

3. Gordon Bowker, *Inside George Orwell—A Biography*, (London: Little, Brown; New York: Palgrave Macmillan, 2003), p. 307.

4. *Orwell—In Front Of Your Nose: The Collected Essays, Journalism & Letters, Volume 4* (Nonpareil Books, 2000), p. 406.

5. Gordon Bowker, *Inside George Orwell—A Biography* (London: Little, Brown; New York: Palgrave Macmillan, 2003), p. 308.

6. George Orwell, *Animal Farm* (New York: Signet Classic, 1990), p. 28.

7. Ibid., p. 28.

8. Ibid., p. 29.

9. Ibid., p. 32.

10. Ibid., p. 37.

11. Ibid., p. 42.

12. Ibid., p. 45.

13. Michael Shelden, *Orwell: The Authorized Biography* (London: Heinemann; New York: HarperCollins, 1991), p. 445.

14. *Animal Farm*, p. 52.

15. Shelden, p. 444.

16. *Animal Farm*, p. 132.

17. Ibid., p. 133.

18. Ibid., p. 139.

19. Gordon Bowker, *Inside George Orwell—A Biography* (London: Little, Brown; New York: Palgrave Macmillan, 2003), pp. 324–325.

20. Bernard Crick, *George Orwell—A Life* (London: Secker and Warburg; Boston: Little, Brown And Company, 1980), p. 325.

21. Michael Shelden, *Orwell: The Authorized Biography* (London: Heinemann; New York: HarperCollins, 1991), p. 449. Also Bernard Crick, *George Orwell—A Life* (London: Secker and Warburg; Boston: Little, Brown And Company, 1980), p. 326.

22. Michael Shelden, *Orwell: The Authorized Biography* (London: Heinemann; New York: HarperCollins, 1991), p. 454. Also Bernard Crick, *George Orwell—A Life* (London: Secker and Warburg; Boston, Little, Brown and Company, 1980), p. 326.

23. Michael Shelden, *Orwell: The Authorized Biography* (London: Heinemann; New York: HarperCollins, 1991), p. 458.

24. George Orwell, "Notes On Nationalism," *Fifty Orwell Essays*, an ebook published by Project Gutenberg of Australia, n.d., <http://www.gutenberg. net.au/pages/orwell> (May 10, 2005).

25. Christopher Hitchens, *Why Orwell Matters* (New York: Basic Books, 2002), p. 104.

26. "English Poetry since 1900," in *George Orwell— The Lost Writings*, ed. W. J. West (New York; Arbor House, first published in Great Britain in 1985), p. 128.

CHAPTER 8. THE YEAR OF DYSTOPIA

1. Michael Shelden, *Orwell: The Authorized Biography* (London: Heinemann; New York: HarperCollins, 1991), p. 511.

2. *Orwell—In Front Of Your Nose: The Collected Essays, Journalism & Letters, Volume 4* (Nonpareil Books, 2000), p. 502.

3. Gordon Bowker, *Inside George Orwell—A Biography* (London: Little, Brown; New York: Palgrave Macmillan, 2003), p. 382.

4. George Orwell, *1984* (New York: Signet Classic, 1990), p. 112.

5. Hilary Spurling, *The Girl from the Fiction Department—A Portrait of Sonia Orwell* (New York: Counterpoint; originally published by Hamish Hamilton, London, 2002), p. 93.

6. Orwell, *1984* (New York: Signet Classic, 1990), p. 24.

7. Ibid., p. 211.

8. Ibid., p. 217.

9. Ibid., p. 218.

10. Ibid., p. 210.

11. Ibid., p. 235.

12. Ibid., p. 245.

13. *George Orwell—The Lost Writings*, ed. W. J. West (New York: Arbor House, first published in Great Britain in 1985), p. 47.

14. Orwell, *1984*, p. 253.

15. "Basic English," *Wikipedia, the Free Encyclopedia*, June 3, 2005, <http://en.wikipedia.org/wiki/Basic_English> (June 10, 2005).

16. Bernard Crick, *George Orwell—A Life* (London: Secker and Warburg; Boston: Little, Brown and Company, 1980), p. 393. Hilary Spurling, *The Girl from the Fiction Department—A Portrait of Sonia Orwell* (New York: Counterpoint, originally published by Hamish Hamilton, London, 2002), p. 166.

17. Bernard Crick, *George Orwell—A Life* (London: Secker and Warburg; Boston: Little, Brown and Company, 1980), p. 393.

CHAPTER 9. THE IMPACT OF ORWELL

1. Michael Shelden, *Orwell: The Authorized Biography* (London: Heinemann; New York: HarperCollins, 1991), p. 505; D. J. Taylor, *Orwell: The Life*, (London: Chatto & Windus; New York: Henry Holt, 2003), p. 418; Gordon Bowker, *Inside George Orwell—A Biography,* (London: Little, Brown; New York: Palgrave Macmillan, 2003), p. 414; Hilary Spurling, *The Girl from the Fiction Department—A Portrait of Sonia Orwell* (New York: Counterpoint, originally published by Hamish Hamilton, London, 2002), p. 98.

2. Bernard Crick, *George Orwell—A Life* (London: Secker and Warburg; Boston: Little, Brown and Company, 1980), p. 392.

3. Hilary Spurling, *The Girl from the Fiction Department—A Portrait of Sonia Orwell* (New York: Counterpoint, 2002), p. 94.

4. Gordon Bowker, *Inside George Orwell—A Biography* (London: Little, Brown; New York: Palgrave Macmillan, 2003), p. 397.

5. Christopher Hitchens, *Why Orwell Matters* (New York: Basic Books, 2002), p. 155.

6. Bernard Crick, *George Orwell—A Life* (London: Secker and Warburg; Boston: Little, Brown and Company, 1980), p. xxix.

7. Hilary Spurling, *The Girl from the Fiction Department—A Portrait of Sonia Orwell* (New York: Counterpoint, 2002), p. 149.

8. Ibid., p. 175.

9. Michael Shelden, *Orwell: The Authorized Biography* (London: Heinemann; New York: HarperCollins, 1991), p. 531.

10. Christopher Hitchens, *Why Orwell Matters* (New York: Basic Books, 2002), p. 174.

11. George Woodcock, *The Crystal Spirit—A Study of George Orwell* (originally published in 1966, new edition 1984; London: Jonathan Cape, 1969), p. 292.

12. Ibid., p. 53.

13. Ibid., p. 3.

GLOSSARY

allegory—A story in which characters and events represent ideas, principles, or forces, so that there is a symbolic meaning in what takes place.

anarchism—The theory or doctrine that all forms of government are oppressive and undesirable and should be abolished.

Big Brother—The mythical, all-knowing leader of the state of Oceania in Orwell's novel *1984*.

capitalism—An economic system in which private individuals and corporations own the means of producing and distributing goods and services and play a major part in controlling wealth.

cold war—A confrontation that stops short of military conflict, such as the classic standoff between the United States with its allies and the Soviet Union and its Communist satellites in the second half of the twentieth century.

communism—A political system of common ownership planned and controlled by the state, based on the Marxist doctrine of revolution by the working class, or proletariat, against capitalism.

communist—A supporter of a communist system or doctrine. Capitalized, a specific government or political party.

doublethink—A term created by Orwell for *1984* and meaning the ability to believe two contradictory ideas at the same time.

dystopia—An imagined world in which authorities have turned people's lives into a nightmare of restrictions and prohibitions.

fable—A story with a moral or purpose that uses animals in place of human characters.

fascism—A political system in which the state controls virtually every aspect of how people live, suppressing opposition, emphasizing conservative values, and typically acting aggressively toward other nations.

fascist—A supporter of a fascist system or doctrine. Capitalized, a specific government or political party.

irony—A word or phrase used with the intention of conveying a meaning different from the literal one, often with the idea of ridiculing the literal meaning.

jargon—Words, phrases, or abbreviations understood

in a specialized field but often meaningless to the general population.

metaphor—A word or phrase used in a nonliteral way in order to suggest a comparison between the thing described and its symbolic qualities.

Newspeak—A version of the English language introduced by the ruling party in *1984* and intended to control people's thoughts by restricting vocabulary.

propaganda—Facts, ideas, and rumors that are spread for the purpose of advancing some political aim or cause.

propagandist—Having to do with propaganda; someone who spreads propaganda.

protagonist—The main character in a work of fiction.

satire—A literary work which exposes vice or folly by making fun of it.

simile—A comparison, usually with "like" or "as," in which the thing being described is understood better by being compared to something with similar qualities.

socialism—A political system in which the community shares power on a relatively equal basis and the state owns means of making and distributing goods. In Marxist theory, the stage that societies go through between capitalism and communism.

socialist—A supporter of a socialist system or doctrine. (Capitalized, a specific government or political party.)

thought crime—A term created by Orwell for *1984* to describe thoughts that the party considered to be wrong.

totalitarianism—A form of government in which the authorities seek to exercise complete control over every aspect of life and tolerate no opposition.

Trotskyism—Named after the Russian revolutionary Leon Trotsky, who believed the working classes should lead a worldwide communist revolution.

utopia—An ideal community, typically considered flawed or impractical by outsiders; derived from a sixteenth-century book written by Sir Thomas More about such a community.

Major Works by George Orwell

Novels:

Burmese Days (1934)

A Clergyman's Daughter (1935)

Keep the Aspidistra Flying (1936)

Coming Up for Air (1939)

Animal Farm (1945)

1984 (1949)

Nonfiction:

Down and Out in Paris and London (1933)

The Road to Wigan Pier (1937)

Homage to Catalonia (1938)

Essays:

"A Hanging" (1931)

"Shooting an Elephant" (1936)

"Down the Mine" (1937)

"North and South" (1937)

"Charles Dickens" (1939)

"Boys' Weeklies" (1940)

"Inside the Whale" (1940)

"The Lion and the Unicorn" (1941)

"Wells, Hitler and the World State" (1941)

"The Art of Donald McGill" (1941)

"Looking Back on the Spanish War" (1943)

"W. B. Yeats" (1943)

"Benefit of Clergy: Some Notes on
Salvador Dali" (1944)

"Arthur Koestler" (1944)

"Notes on Nationalism" (1945)

"How the Poor Die" (1946)

"Politics vs. Literature: An Examination of
Gulliver's Travels" (1946)

"Politics and the English Language" (1946)

"Second Thoughts on James Burnham"
1946)

"Decline of the English Murder" (1946)

"Some Thoughts on the Common Toad"
(1946)

"A Good Word for the Vicar of Bray" (1946)

"In Defence of P. G. Wodehouse" (1946)

"Why I Write" (1946)

"The Prevention of Literature" (1946)

"Such, Such Were the Joys" (1946)

"Lear, Tolstoy and the Fool" (1947)

"Writers And Leviathan" (1948)

"Reflections on Gandhi" (1949)

FURTHER READING

Agathocleous, Tanya. *George Orwell: Battling Big Brother.* New York: Oxford University Press, 2000.

Bloom, Harold, ed. *George Orwell's* 1984. Broomall, Pa.: Chelsea House, 2004.

Bowker, Gordon. *Inside George Orwell: A Biography.* New York: Macmillan, 2003.

Brunsdale, Mitzi M. *Student Companion to George Orwell.* Westport, Conn.: Greenwood Press, 2000.

Cushman, Thomas, and John Rodden, eds. *George Orwell: Into The Twenty-first Century.* New York: Paradigm Publishers, 2005.

Internet Addresses

George Orwell Resources
http://students.ou.edu/C/Kara.C.Chiodo-1/orwell.html

George Orwell (1903–1950)
http://www.levity.com/corduroy/orwell.htm

The George Orwell Web Ring
http://www.netcharles.com/orwell/ext/206.htm

INDEX